PUFFIN

CRIC

Diptakirti Chaudhuri has been a sa
He was born and brought up in Calcutta but currently lives and works in Gurgaon. He loves books, trivia and books on trivia. His blog, Calcutta Chromosome, can be found at http://diptakirti.blogspot.com.

He is married with a four-year-old son. This is his first book.

CRICKET!
All You Wanted to Know About the WORLD CUP

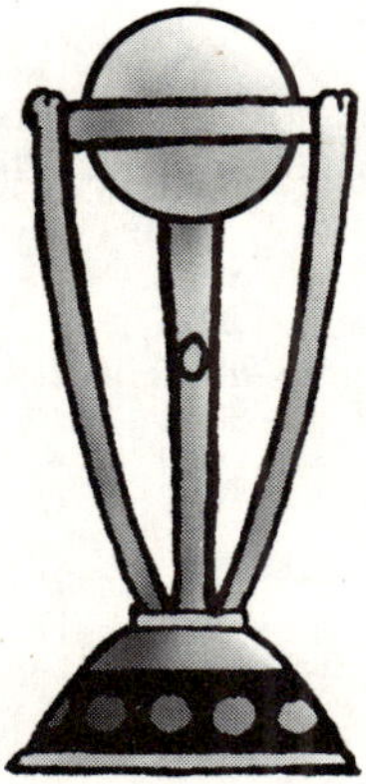

Diptakirti Chaudhuri

Illustrations by
Dipankar Bhattacharya

PUFFIN BOOKS

PUFFIN BOOKS
Published by the Penguin Group
Penguin Books India Pvt. Ltd, 11 Community Centre, Panchsheel Park, New Delhi 110 017, India
Penguin Group (USA) Inc., 375 Hudson Street, New York, New York 10014, USA
Penguin Group (Canada), 90 Eglinton Avenue East, Suite 700, Toronto, Ontario, M4P 2Y3, Canada (a division of Pearson Penguin Canada Inc.)
Penguin Books Ltd, 80 Strand, London WC2R 0RL, England
Penguin Ireland, 25 St Stephen's Green, Dublin 2, Ireland (a division of Penguin Books Ltd)
Penguin Group (Australia), 250 Camberwell Road, Camberwell, Victoria 3124, Australia (a division of Pearson Australia Group Pty Ltd)
Penguin Group (NZ), 67 Apollo Drive, Rosedale, North Shore 0632, New Zealand (a division of Pearson New Zealand Ltd)
Penguin Group (South Africa) (Pty) Ltd, 24 Sturdee Avenue, Rosebank, Johannesburg 2196, South Africa

Penguin Books Ltd, Registered Offices: 80 Strand, London WC2R 0RL, England

First published in Puffin by Penguin Books India 2011

10 9 8 7 6 5 4 3 2 1

ISBN 9780143331612

Typeset in Adobe Caslon Pro by InoSoft Systems
Printed at Manipal Press Ltd, Manipal

Acknowledgements

This book could not have been written without the wonderful website called Cricinfo.com which provides information, knowledge and perspective, not necessarily in that order.

Thanks are also due to:

- Udayan Chakrabarti and Soumya Bhattacharya, who read an interim draft of the book and gave valuable feedback.
- Sudeep Lahiri, for being the book's most enthusiastic supporter. Any cricket team would be delighted to have such a fan.
- Sudeshna Shome Ghosh, for making the offer I couldn't refuse. Maybe we will speak one day.
- Rita Chaudhuri, for the genes.
- Trishna and Dyujoy Chaudhuri, for providing inspiration and instigation. And allowing me the use of the laptop.

This book is dedicated to Debapriya Chaudhuri—who would have been the 'happiest person'.

Contents

The Story Till Now

The Cup Quest

Odds and Ends

PART A

The Story Till Now

1.

The Beginning of Cricket

It all started some time in the 16th century in Britain. It was then a game where one person tried to hit a three-legged stool with a leather ball while another player stood in front of it, trying to hit the ball away, first with bare hands and then with a wooden plank. Often they used a wicket gate instead of the stool as the target to defend. (That's probably why whenever a person gets out in cricket, we get 'his wicket'.)

So how did the name 'cricket' come about? Leave it to the scholars and you have a million, totally spaced out options—none of them coming close to what the game was then or what it is now.

Here are three options. Close your eyes and tap on one. That's your choice for how the name 'cricket' came about!

1. cricc or cryce: crutch or staff in Old English (for the thing that they played the game with)
2. kricke: a stick in Middle Dutch (as above)
3. met de krik ketsen: 'with the stick chase' in Middle Dutch (Why? Oh why?)

As lots of small and big boys started playing, the game changed and brought the original game closer to the version we recognize today.

When bowlers started coming too close to the batsman, the pitch length was fixed (at 22 yards). When batsmen used planks that were too wide, the maximum dimensions of a bat were defined. And fielders were disallowed to use their hats to catch balls!

Very soon, actually not very soon, in about two hundred years, (around 1755) the Laws of Cricket were created. Mind you, they are not rules governing some silly game. They are Laws. They are the very basis of life!

In between, during the 18th century, cricket had travelled to all the colonies of England—West Indies, North America, India, Australia, New Zealand and South Africa—when trading and political set-ups were being created there. So now you know what is common between all (or most) of the cricket-playing countries today—they are former British colonies.

Gradually, most of these countries developed some skill and love for the game. Enough to start *testing* their strength in a contest with England. And hence the name, Test cricket.

2.

Test Cricket
(*or International Cricket*)

The first two international teams to play a game of cricket were USA and Canada in 1844. In New York. Obviously, the proximity helped. The Canadians probably came over in a wagon and had the match.

On the other hand, Australia was forty-eight days away (by sea, since British Airways was some time away!) from England. Any cricket in either of these countries meant at least three months of travel before one could squeeze in a day's play!

Despite that, an official English team toured Australia in March 1877 and played the first Test match in the history of cricket. Australian opener Charles Bannerman cornered pretty much all the pioneering records like the first run, the first dropped catch and everything in between to become the first centurion as well.

The honours were quite evenly spread out in the first few years. In

1882, only one Test was played when Australia toured England in which England chased 85 in the last innings and lost! After that defeat, a mock obituary came out in the *Sporting Times*:

> In Affectionate Remembrance
> OF
> **ENGLISH CRICKET,**
> WHICH DIED AT THE OVAL
> ON
> 29th August, 1882,
> Deeply lamented by a large circle of sorrowing friends and acquantances
>
> R. I. P.
>
> *N.B.-. The body will be cremated and the ashes taken to Australia.*

That was how the oldest cricketing rivalry got a name.

From then onwards, getting 'Test' status became the final achievement of a nation playing cricket. Only ten teams have achieved that in the last 130 years or so.

Some people think five long days of cricket is a waste of time. Others feel it is the ultimate test of cricketing ability. In Tests sometimes you have to cut loose and score a century before lunch. Sometimes you need to hang in there and score 30 runs in one session. The beauty of Test cricket is, both these innings can win you the match!

3.

One Day Internationals

The first international one-day match was played to pacify irate spectators.

1971, Melbourne: After three rain-washed days, the crowd was thoroughly miffed at the wet, cricket-less beginning to the new year. The Australian Cricket Board decided to have a 40-over game (of 8 balls each) against the visiting English team. Australian players—who had no experience of limited-overs cricket—must have been really surprised to see nearly 50,000 people walk in to watch this match. And they surprised the spectators by going on to win it! Like the first ever international Test match, the first ODI also went to the Aussies.

The England players would have been less surprised at the spontaneous audience reaction because they had been playing limited-overs domestic tournaments for nearly a decade. Top international cricketers from South Africa and West Indies toured England throughout the 1960s to play some fast-paced matches. To keep the action fast, bowling run-ups were restricted to 15 yards in these matches. Several sponsors had also come on board, which is always a sure sign of popularity!

Even without the international players, English counties regularly played these games on Sunday afternoons. BBC aired the matches live and the first cricket couch-potatoes were born.

Despite the popularity of this version of the game in England, other countries were relatively slower in adopting this format. In fact, only eighty-two ODI games (despite two World Cups) were played in the 1970s—a majority of which involved England, Australia and the West Indies.

The first World Cup happened in 1975 and that made the format more global. Towards the end of the decade, more interesting stuff started happening like day-and-night matches and coloured clothing, as more and more people got addicted.

Then in 1983, India, a rank outsider, won the World Cup against all odds. And a billion people got hooked!

4.

Twenty20

ODI cricket went all over the world. One of the most unlikely—but popular—venues was Sharjah, for its high-voltage India-Pakistan clashes egged on by expatriates of both countries settled in UAE. ODIs were the favourites of spectators in the 1980s and 1990s.

Just as ODI cricket gained popularity when people were thinking five-day Tests were a bit of a drag, people started thinking the same of one-day cricket by the 2000s. One *full* day of watching cricket and doing nothing? You can do 242 Facebook updates in that time! Can we get something that gets over a little quicker?

So, the good guys at ECB (England & Wales Cricket Board) cut down ODIs by 60 per cent and gave us a game that could get over in an evening. People could get out of work a little early, go over to the stadium and watch a game of cricket in about the same time it takes to watch a movie.

To make the game even faster, pavilions were done away with. Players sat in baseball-style dugouts and incoming batsmen had to be at the wicket within a minute of the dismissal. Add to that, cheerleaders, DJs, fielders with mikes (giving interviews during matches), longer periods of fielding restrictions and you had a new format of cricket that had spectators wearing hard hats at its first World Cup—due to the raining sixes!

The purists frowned at this slam-bang version because it threatened to undermine the need for playing technically sound cricket. The positive side was that it put a higher premium on fitness, seeking younger players. But like most predictions, both of these were turned on their head. In IPL 2010, three out of the

top four run-getters turned out to be more than thirty-five years in age and were established Test batsmen—Sachin Tendulkar, Jacques Kallis and Sourav Ganguly.

In T20s, it hardly matters who gets the runs as long as they come in fours and sixes; there is music accompanying each boundary and newer sections of people started falling in love with the game because of these.

After all, T20 was launched in 2003 by ECB with the slogan 'I don't like cricket. I love it!'

5.

Crickertainment

Imagine a game of cricket where the teams are not national. They play day-and-night matches wearing coloured clothing. There are ladies serving drinks during the breaks. There is heavy advertising of the matches. The matches are shown on channels that are not traditional sports channels.

Sounds familiar? Been seeing all of these at the Indian Premier League?

Well, these things first happened more than thirty years back! And again in India, a few years ago.

The reason behind both these attempts at jazzing up cricket was related to disagreements around TV broadcasting rights. Both were planned by two millionaires from Australia and India respectively. In 1977, Kerry Packer started World Series Cricket. In 2007, Subhash Chandra (of the Zee Group) started Indian Cricket League (ICL).

Both these businessmen started these 'rebel' cricket leagues when they were denied the rights to air international cricket matches. Packer went around the globe and offered big money to international stars to play in what he called World Series Cricket (WSC). Since the normal fees of cricketers were not very high at that time, he attracted the best in the world, players like Tony Greig, Clive Lloyd, Greg Chappell, Dennis Lillee, Imran Khan and Andy Roberts.

Subhash Chandra tapped the large pool of Indian domestic cricketers, who were again paid very poorly, as well as some near-retirement international stars to start the Indian Cricket League (ICL).

Both events were heavily advertised. There was lots of entertainment and drama apart from cricket. Kerry Packer's WSC was also the first to start many of the TV viewing add-ons like multi-cam set-ups and stump-mikes. In both cases, the cricket boards were angry enough to blacklist the players and drop them from the national teams.

WSC was a runaway success and grew to become a much-awaited tournament. Seeing its success, the Australian Cricket Board had to negotiate with Packer to give him the cricket broadcasting rights and the World Series became an official tournament.

ICL had a moderate run, was aired on Zee channels and promoted well but the lack of really big stars hurt the viewership. Meanwhile the BCCI got its act together and came up with the IPL. With the entire Indian national team coming on board and the regional passion of city teams, IPL has gone on to become the richest, buzziest and the most controversial in a span of only three years.

IPL is now a part of our cricketing lives. We look forward to it around April every year and think it is the greatest blend of fun and games that could have happened.

It is. Except that the idea is not original. It is just bigger.

MOTHER OF ALL COINCIDENCES

Some very crazy things have happened during cricket matches. Here are two stories of coincidences that are so strange that if they had been shown in a film, we would have laughed at the improbability of it all!

BEEN THERE, DONE THAT

In 1956, ten-year-old Richard Stokes was taken to the Old Trafford cricket ground to watch an Ashes match. Richard's memories of that match are vague as he only remembers that there were an awful lot of spectators for a cold, wet day. He also remembers that the crowd was very excited because a right-arm off-spinner was running through the Aussies. This was no exaggeration because the off-spinner, Jim Laker, took each of the 10 wickets that fell in that innings (and nine of the other innings as well).

Forty-three years later, Mr Stokes was in Delhi on work and he heard about India playing Pakistan at Feroze Shah Kotla. Since he was now based out of Germany, he did not want to miss out on watching some live cricket and managed to get a ticket. Mr Stokes reached the ground after lunch (on the last day of the match) and saw yet another bowler running through the opposition. As Anil Kumble took 10 wickets—the only time a bowler has done this after Laker—Richard Stokes became a part of the magnificent record held by two bowlers half a century apart.

He was there at both places, the only person on the planet to have seen a single bowler take ten wickets in an innings. Live.

A HUNDRED YEARS

Australia and England played, in 1877, what became the first ever Test match. Thanks to a century from Charles Bannerman who ended up scoring two-thirds of his team's runs, Australia had a decent score (245 runs) in the first innings. After England scored 196 and conceded a lead, both the teams had a collapse in their second innings. Australia ended up winning the game by 45 runs.

Australia 245 (Bannerman 165) and 104 beat England 196 (Jupp 63, Charlwood 36) and 108 by 45 runs.

A hundred years after the match, Australia and England met again at the same venue (Melbourne Cricket Ground) to play The Centenary Test. Batting first, Australia had a mini collapse in their first innings, which was matched by a mega-collapse in England's first. Australia turned around in the second innings to put up a substantial score, leaving England to get 463 to win. England ended up—you guessed it—45 runs short.

Australia 138 (Greg Chappell 40) and 419 (Rodney Marsh 110, Davis 68, Walters 66, Hookes 56) beat England 95 and 417 (Derek Randall 174, Denniss Amiss 64) by 45 runs.

6.

The Gods of Cricket

The last four decades in which ODIs have been played have seen cut-throat competition. Most of the teams have been quite evenly matched and close matches have been plentiful. Last ball wins have been one of the reasons why ODIs pack in the crowds whenever they are played.

In fact, the hallmark of this version of cricket has been the equality of teams. Rank outsiders like India and Sri Lanka have won World Cups, as have pre-tournament favourites like West Indies and Australia. There have been upsets galore as virtually every team has lost to a first-timer during some tournament or the other.

In 2011, as we cheer India as a potential No. 1, we also need to watch the very closely bunched together teams of South Africa, England, Pakistan and Sri Lanka in the rankings. With technology, modern training methods, awareness about fitness levels, the gap between countries is reducing. By and large, all teams are now equal. In the ODI World Cup, we are looking for the first among equals.

What follows is a tribute to two teams who have been the undisputed No. 1 at ODIs at various points of time and two more who were the challengers.

ENGLAND

The country which started it all—cricket as well as one-day cricket—was also among the early leaders. In the 1970s, England had impressive Test batsmen who adapted well to the new format.

Their bowlers, like Bob Willis and Ian Botham, had the pace and the attitude. Most importantly, the ODI format was adopted by the English County Championship and the newer players got accustomed to it quickly.

England, however, lacked two things. One, a captain who could lead the team unequivocally and energise them towards a grand vision and secondly, a steady stream of raw talent. It has always had a competent team but not a wildly talented one.

England had its best winning ratio in the 1970s, post which it has gone steadily downhill. This could be attributed to their being more accustomed to the game initially, but the advantage wore off once other nations caught on.

	Played	Won	Lost	W/L Ratio
1970s	46	27	15	1.80
1980s	120	64	55	1.16
1990s	135	60	70	0.86
2000s	224	100	111	0.90

England has been the runners-up at the World Cup three times (1979, 1987 and 1992) but has never won it.

They are the reigning world champions of T20, and the current team (which has a very impressive record in Tests also) could well be the team which gets England its first ODI World Cup.

WEST INDIES

At one point of time, the West Indies team was bursting at the seams with batting talent. But despite their great batting line-up, what set them apart was their battery of fast bowlers. Traditionally, fast bowlers played in pairs. With West Indies, it was a quartet.

Their pace battery was not an accidental discovery but a long-term strategy of their visionary captain, Clive Lloyd. He combined the natural strengths of a West Indian cricketer with the general discomfort of batsmen towards genuine pace to develop a bowling machine that decimated every batting line-up in the world. With fearsome bowlers like Malcolm Marshall, Michael Holding, Joel Garner, Andy Roberts, Colin Croft, Courtney Walsh, Patrick Patterson and Curtley Ambrose, West Indies seemed to have an assembly line of fast bowlers.

Imagine a day's batting in which every ball could crack your skull. If the body didn't give way, the mind did!

Countries like India, which did not have fast pitches, had the poorest record against them but they were not an exception. Clive Lloyd's West Indies defeated almost every country at home and away to build a winning streak (of eleven matches), which was broken nearly two decades later, by Steve Waugh's Australia.

Interestingly, this world-beating team did not have any 'coach' at the peak of their prowess.

Once the extremely talented bunch of pacers started retiring, their team strength dwindled. Also, new rules restricted the number of short-pitched deliveries in an over and curbed fast bowling across the world. West Indies went into a decline from the 1990s and their current record is a rather sad reminder of their glorious days.

	ODIs Played	Won	Lost	W/L Ratio
1970s	23	17	6	2.83
1980s	170	122	46	2.65
1990s	195	96	89	1.08
2000s	232	94	123	0.76

West Indies played 82 Tests in the 1980s. They won 43 of them and lost only 8, which is a win-loss ratio of 5.4—something that has not been touched even by current-day Australia.

AUSTRALIA

We did not know it then, but Australia started its march towards world dominance with the 1987 World Cup, which it won a tad unexpectedly. Under Allan Border's captaincy and Bobby Simpson's coaching, it started moving towards a level very few countries have achieved in team sports.

Mentioning the coach of 1987 is important because the captain and coach combination has always been vital in the Aussie game-plan. Coaches like Bobby Simpson and John Buchanan have been critical to their successes, providing a strategic edge to their formidable cricketing skills.

Australia was one of the first teams to add physical fitness as a vital factor to its winning strategy. Their fielding, not to mention catching, and running between the wickets routinely saved or added runs that often turned out to be the difference between winning and losing.

Leadership, stable and mature, came in the form of Allan Border, Mark Taylor, Steve Waugh and Ricky Ponting. All of them have led, often through personal example, a team of extremely talented people.

Apart from that, Australians excelled at what they called 'mental disintegration'. Taking the 'winning' motive as paramount, they thought nothing of 'sledging' opposition players on the field, unsettling them through aggressive body language and starting the battle much before the game began by taking potshots at the opposition through the media.

Thanks to their confidence (some called it arrogance), passion (aggression) and strong leaders, Australia is also the team everyone loves to hate. Whenever any team has come close to challenging the Aussie dominance, there has been a lot of support for the other team. Call it the love for the underdog or the dislike for the 'ugly Aussie', nobody really likes an arrogant topper!

INDIA

If data is checked, India has never come anywhere near the No. 1 position *consistently*. We have been No. 1 in Test ranking but let's face it, both Australia and South Africa have always been within sniffing distance of the spot. And yet, if there is a team that has pulled off the most spectacular successes against the strongest of teams, it has been India.

Funnily enough, India's biggest strength has been its population. Thanks to that, a large bunch of insanely talented players turn up at regular intervals and become the mainstay behind India's performances. Over the years, coaching has been able to bring some finesse to the raw talent, but the dependence has mainly been on the individual talent of the stars.

Speaking of coaching, foreign coaches have had chequered stints in India. Two—John Wright and Gary Kirsten—have been successful, while Greg Chappell had a forgettable stint. That's strange because of the three, Chappell had the most accomplished international career. And yet, his 'Aussie' way of handling things probably put off the Indian cricketers. The coaches who managed to 'nudge' the Indian players rather than 'push' them have been successful in India.

India has become a contender for the No.1 spot probably because its playing record has consistently crept up in successive decades.

	1970s	1980s	1990s	2000s
W/L Ratios of Tests	0.89	0.52	0.90	1.48
W/L Ratios of ODIs	0.18	0.86	1.02	1.24

The 70s were a complete disaster.

In the 80s, we had a decently talented team and improved.

In the 90s and 2000s, the team got leadership stability. Starting with Mohammed Azharuddin, followed by Sourav Ganguly and now Mahendra Singh Dhoni, each Indian captain has managed to break the records of his illustrious predecessor. And that's not a bad thing at all!

TEAM NAMES

INDIA

The Indian cricket team has always played in blue jerseys, starting from the mid-1980s when the World Series Cricket in Australia introduced coloured clothing. The shade of blue, however, changed over the years from light blue to dark and back again. The designs also changed from tournament to tournament with things like yellow horizontal stripes, splashes of the tricolour appearing on the uniform. Before the 2003 World Cup, Pepsi launched an advertising campaign called Men In Blue and the name stuck, becoming popular in everyday usage.

The blue-ness of the Indian team is set to be further cemented as Nike has launched a campaign for the 2011 World Cup—Bleed Blue.

AUSTRALIA

Right from the time they started playing international cricket, Australian cricketers wore a distinctive green cap. Instead of fitting tightly, like most sports caps, this one was slightly loose and became known as the Baggy Green. This cap, by which an Australian cricket player is identified and often referred to, is a very important symbol. Getting the 'Baggy Green' on the morning of one's first international match involves a ceremonial handing over of the cap either by the captain or a past Australian player.

The way people who represent their universities in some sport in Britain are called 'Blues', the Australian cricketers are sometimes called 'Baggy Greens'.

SOUTH AFRICA

The flower at the centre of the Cricket South Africa crest is the protea—the country's national flower and this is the name, Proteas, by which all South African sports teams are identified, except for the rugby team which is called the Springboks.

Incidentally, Springboks (literally, 'jumping antelope') was also the name by which all South African sports teams were known, since it is also the national animal of the country. However, as it was the symbol used during Apartheid, it was changed to Proteas after Nelson Mandela's government came to power.

NEW ZEALAND

Why the New Zealand cricketers are called the Black Caps is easy enough to explain! Not only is the cap of the current team black, so is the rest of the uniform.

All Blacks is a nickname for all New Zealand sports teams because of their uniform. It is used most widely for their successful rugby team. The cricket team is probably not called All Blacks because for most of the 1980s, they wore a beige uniform. In fact, a group of New Zealand supporters call themselves the Beige Brigade and identify themselves by wearing that colour.

SUPPORTERS

One of the most well-known supporter groups in cricket is the Barmy Army, which is a vocal and visibly organized group of English cricket fans. They never indulge in any unsavoury behaviour (unlike English soccer fans, for example) but are known for their loud and audacious chanting (even when their team is losing)!

Borrowing their name, Indian supporters in overseas matches have christened themselves Bharat Army and are almost as vocal.

7.

Cricketing Rivalries

Nothing is more exciting on a cricket field than a fast bowler charging in and delivering a scorching bouncer that zips past the batsman's chin. The drama doesn't always end there, though.

Sometimes you have the fast bowler rushing up to the batsman after the bouncer and throwing a barb or two. Suddenly the game of cricket transforms. It is no longer a friendly game of bat and ball. The teams transform into two gladiators facing each other in a fight unto death. Add to that historical subtexts like colonial relationships, shared political boundaries and you have all the makings of war.

Indeed, cricket has been called War Minus the Shooting.

Here is a look at two teams who have fought each other bitterly on the cricket field. The battles have been personal. The acrimony palpable. And there was too much other than cricket happening. But it was gripping stuff. You couldn't take your eyes off it while it happened!

INDIA VS PAKISTAN

'*Pyar to hona hi tha*'. During India's historic 2004 tour of Pakistan, this banner came up in the stands. It symbolized the Indo-Pak rivalry very well. Bitter rivalry interspersed with effusive gestures has been the hallmark of these two countries separated at birth, and that charges the atmosphere like nothing else.

Add to that the relatively low number of matches played between them, due to politics, and the stakes go even higher. Supporters from both sides have often said that it did not matter if their team lost a tournament as long as they defeated the other.

Both the teams have been blessed with great talent down the ages and that has led to nail-biting contests. Pakistan is considered to be the fount of some exceptional fast bowlers, among the best in the world. India, quite symmetrically, is home to some of the best batsmen of modern cricket. Be it Imran Khan versus Sunil Gavaskar or Sachin Tendulkar versus Shoaib Akhtar, the competition has always been intense in an India-Pakistan match.

In the playing history of the two countries, three matches can be identified at which there has been a shift of momentum. These matches have come about a decade apart and have been representative of the cricket that was played in the subsequent years.

In the initial years of ODIs (till April 1986), very little ODI cricket was played between India and Pakistan and the honours were equally shared.

Year	Total Matches	India Win	Pakistan Win	No Result	India Win %
Till 17 April 1986	16	8	7	1	50%

18 April 1986: In Sharjah, the finals of the Australasia Cup saw the first tectonic shift. Javed Miandad hit a six off the last ball of the match when four runs were required. With that one shot, Javed Miandad tilted the balance decisively in Pakistan's favour for nearly a decade. Whenever Pakistan played India, they seemed to have a psychological edge that often weakened a superior-on-paper Indian team. Especially in Sharjah (the venue of that shot), India had a terrible record against them.

India (245/7 in 50 overs, K. Srikkanth 75 in 80 balls, Sunil Gavaskar 92) lost to Pakistan (248/9 in 50 overs, Javed Miandad 116 in 114 balls).

Year	Total Matches	India Win	Pakistan Win	No Result	India Win %
18 April 1986 to 8 March 1996	25	4	20	1	16%

9 March 1996: India defeated Pakistan in an electrifying World Cup quarter-final with Ajay Jadeja playing the innings of a lifetime (where he scored a whirlwind 45 off 25 balls). The Pakistani middle-order was not able to capitalize on a blistering opening partnership and collapsed. In a very symbolic result, India beat Pakistan in what was Javed Miandad's last ODI. Till the moment he was there, there seemed to be hope for Pakistan, however hopeless the Required Run Rate looked. With his departure in a run-out, India swung the momentum, not only of the match but for future face-offs as well.

India (287/8 in 50 overs, N.S. Sidhu 93, Ajay Jadeja 45 in 25 balls) defeated Pakistan (248/9 in 49 overs, Saeed Anwar 48 in 32 balls, Aamer Sohail 55 in 46 balls).

Year	Total Matches	India Win	Pakistan Win	No Result	India Win %
9 March 1996 to 28 February 2003	44	17	25	2	39%

1 March 2003: This was yet another World Cup match billed as a battle between Sachin Tendulkar and Shoaib Akhtar. It was settled in the second over of the Indian innings when the Master Blaster derailed the Rawalpindi Express.

18 runs came off the over (1w-0-1-0-2w-6-4-4) and it gave India enough momentum to tide over some mid-inning jitters to win yet another battle of nerves. After Sachin's departure, Rahul Dravid and Yuvraj Singh took India to victory quite easily, with nearly 5 overs to spare.

Pakistan (273/7 in 50 overs, Saeed Anwar 101, Zaheer Khan 10-0-46-2) lost to India (276/4 in 45.4 overs, Tendulkar 98 in 75 balls, Yuvraj 50, Dravid 44*)*

Year	Total Matches	India Win	Pakistan Win	No Result	India Win %
1 March 2003 to end-2009	33	16	17	0	50%

Post this match, there was one more movement of the momentum towards India as its success record improved. Also, with more and more matches being played between the countries, the camaraderie improved.

The pressure to win is still there and a match with Pakistan still has that must-win edge. But we enjoy it more!

CRICKETING PEOPLE

Cricket has had many greats who have defined the way the game is played. There was Bradman, whose batting averages are still beyond realms of possibility. There was Jardine, whose ruthless captaincy during the 1932–'33 'Bodyline' series almost brought down diplomatic relationships between England and Australia. There is Tendulkar, whose mastery over all forms of the game is quite unparalleled. There is Warne, who single-handedly rejuvenated the art of leg spin.

But what about the people who have become part of the game?

Here are five people, whose contributions to the game became cricketing terms.

Bosie: This is a term for what we know as the googly, an off-break ball (which deviates from off to leg) delivered by a right-arm leg-spinner. Though rarely used now, this term came from the name of B.J.T. Bosanquet, an English bowler who was very good at this delivery.

Bradmanesque: For batting averages that are unbelievably high, named after Donald Bradman who ended his 52-Test career with an average of 99.94.

Chinaman: A ball from a left-handed leg-spinner that breaks from off to leg (to a right-handed batsman) basically, a left-handed leg-spinner's googly! This is said to be named after Ellis Achong, a West Indian bowler of Chinese descent.

Dilscoop a.k.a. Dilshan Scoop: The now-popular T20 shot which is like a vertical sweep shot as the batsman kneels down to scoop a ball over the wicketkeeper's head. This is named after Sri Lankan batsman, Tillakaratne Dilshan, who popularized it during the 2009 World T20 tournament.

Mankaded: A form of dismissal in which the incoming bowler runs the non-striker out if he has left his crease to get a run. This is named after Indian all-rounder, Vinoo Mankad, who did it twice on a tour to Australia. While legitimate by the laws of cricket, this form of dismissal is considered unsporting if the bowler does not warn the batsman once first.

Sidhuism: An inane one-liner that is borrowed from an English idiom and made to connect with a cricketing situation. E.g. 'He has thrown a drowning man both ends of a rope' when talking about a call for a run that led to a run-out. Named after Navjyot Sidhu, former Indian opener, cricket commentator, TV show judge and Indian Member of Parliament.

8.

Changing Records

Cricket is changing. Oh yeah? Like you needed *me* to tell you that!

You know, people who have watched cricket in the 1980s would remember Krishnamachari Srikkanth[1] as a swashbuckling batsman, who thought nothing of trying to hit the first ball of the day for a six. In many ways, he was the first 'pinch-hitter'—pushing up the run rate in the initial overs. But when you flip through record-books (actually, record websites), you realize Srikkanth has a career strike rate of 72 in ODIs. While he scored at a pace of 72 runs per 100 balls in the faster version of the game, Virender Sehwag has a strike rate of 81 in *Tests*. Whoa!

And before you say that Sehwag is a bit of a madcap himself—scoring boundaries at will—I will quickly lay out a table of numbers.

Take the last two decades. Break them into five-year chunks. Take the Top 5 batsmen of each period. And what do you see?

	1990-94	1995-99	2000-04	2005-09
Batting average	39.5	41.2	39.1	43.2
Strike Rate	74.5	76.1	80.8	91.1

The batting averages remain more or less in the same zone (about 40) but those runs have been scored at a much faster pace—nearly 25 per cent faster! Double whoa!

[1] *Present-day fans would know Srikkanth as the Chairman of Selectors and a very vocal fan of Chennai Super Kings in the Indian Premier League.*

END OF BOREDOM

A new format of cricket always comes in when the earlier format gets predictable. ODI cricket started at a time, 1970s, when 5-day Test cricket was seen to be too long. Captains were perfectly happy to 'bat out' oppositions and secure dull draws.

So, when a whole lot of jazzy ODI championships popped up in the 1980s, everybody thought Test cricket would now die out. But as it turned out, this was actually a blessing in disguise for Test cricket.

As the frequency of ODI matches increased, the slam-bang style started appearing in Test cricket as well. Players stepped up the tempo in Test cricket, as more and more matches started having results.

A table tracking the number of Tests played in each decade clearly picks up this trend.

	1960s	1970s	1980s	1990s	2000s
Tests played	186	198	266	347	464
Results obtained	97	114	143	223	350
In %	52%	58%	54%	64%	75%
Runs per over	2.49	2.69	2.86	2.86	3.20

From the 1960s to the 1980s, results happened in only about half the matches. Runs scored were at a sedate pace of 2.7 runs per over. The run rate saw a jump in nearly every decade and in the 2000s, three-fourths of the matches had a result.

Moreover, the funniest is that the number of Test matches being played is also increasing. Lots of people had predicted that Test cricket would die out. But that doesn't seem to have happened.

More ODIs are being played now. So are more Test matches. More and more people are watching all the versions and newer fans come into the games, expecting to see more stuff.

And ODI has taken the boredom out of Test cricket as well!

9.

6.6.6.6.6.6

For all the jumps in scoring rates, one record remains quite exclusive. It has happened only four times—twice in first-class cricket and twice in international cricket. Many people have come close, but here are the four who have actually hit six sixes in one over.

NOTTINGHAMSHIRE VS GLAMORGAN, ENGLISH COUNTY LEAGUE 1968

Garfield Sobers, one of world's greatest all-rounders, was leading Nottinghamshire. At the end of Day One, Sobers wanted some quick runs on the board before he put Glamorgan in for the last few overs of the day.

Quick runs he got as Malcolm Nash, a left-arm seamer, tried some slow bowling to Sobers. Bad move.

Except for one hit which a fielder caught and toppled over the ropes, all the sixes landed either in the stands or outside the ground. The last ball was recovered by a boy from the streets the next day and it is now in a museum. Nobody looked for it because Sobers declared immediately after he got the 36.

Malcolm Nash has 991 first-class wickets to his credit. And one bad over eclipsed all that.

BOMBAY VS BARODA, RANJI TROPHY WEST ZONE LEAGUE 1984-85

In a slightly sleepy domestic match, Bombay wanted some quick runs in its second innings before it let Baroda bat. All-rounder Ravi Shastri took it upon himself to push up the scoring rate and while doing so, broke a million records. 13 sixes, fastest double-century, super-fast century and, of course, 36 runs off an over from Tilak Raj.

This Baroda all-rounder had a decent match otherwise. He scored 55 and 28 (opening the batting) and got Sunil Gavaskar's wicket in the second innings. But we remember only that over.

SOUTH AFRICA VS NETHERLANDS, ICC ODI WORLD CUP 2007

Herschelle Gibbs was the man who did it first in international cricket. One could argue that Netherlands was not much better than any county side but the fact of the matter is that Gibbs did it at the World Cup.

At 178/2 in 29 overs, South Africa was cruising towards a big score. How big the score could be wasn't clear till Dan Van Bunge's fourth over was bowled.

Equally distributing the shots between long on and long off, Gibbs helped himself to 36 runs in the first international version of this achievement.

INDIA VS ENGLAND, ICC T20 WORLD CUP 2007

The second time it happened in an international match, there were no minnows involved. And the stage was huge—the first T20 World Cup.

Yuvraj Singh was batting on 14, when he was taunted by Andrew Flintoff. Yuvraj retorted and umpires intervened to resume peaceful play. But not as peaceful as Stuart Broad, bowler of over no. 19, would have liked!

Mid-wicket. Backward square leg. Extra cover. Backward point. Mid-wicket. Long on.

India went from 171/3 to 207/3 in six balls as Yuvraj Singh reached 50 (in 12 balls) from 14 (in 6) to hit the fastest T20 half-century. Strike rate of 417. Beat that!

So, do you think anybody will do it again in this World Cup? Will they do it against one of the newer teams? Or, will somebody be able to do the 'impossible' and hit seven sixes in an over? And who will be the bowler who makes it possible by bowling a no-ball?

10.

The Cup of Joy

1975 AND 1979, ENGLAND

What was the big deal? When the decision was taken to have a Cricket World Cup, noted cricket writer Tony Cozier wrote, 'perhaps the boldest and most ambitious innovation the game has known since the legalization of over-arm bowling'. Wow!

Of course, a world championship of Test matches would have taken till half-past forever, so when the ODI format started, people jumped at having the grand event.

The only thing that wasn't a very big deal was the prize money. The winning *team* got £ 4,000, which is about what any Indian cricketer gets to play a *single* ODI today!

What else? The first two World Cups were similar in many respects. Both of them happened in England (the only place where it could have happened). They were quickly over (eight teams in two groups, who played each other once, and four proceeded to the semis). And they were both won by West Indies.

So, West Indies won? Quite emphatically. Except for a no-result in a match against Sri Lanka (1979), they won all their matches in the first two World Cups. In the first, they defeated Australia in the final. In the second, it was England. In the first, captain Clive Lloyd scored a century. In the second, it was Viv Richards (considered by many as the best batsman of the times). Add to that their pace battery and you almost had a cakewalk.

How did India do? Quite disastrously. In the first edition they managed to defeat only East Africa, the babes of cricket. In the second, they managed to lose all three matches, including one to minnows Sri Lanka. The joke was that India played for draws, even in ODIs!

1983, ENGLAND

What was the big deal? Nothing, to start with. The third World Cup started with an air of the inevitable. Clive Lloyd's world-beating West Indians were scheduled to pick up their third trophy and the rest of the countries were supposed to go through the motions. The big deal was the country which met them in the final.

What else? Well, the format and the number of countries remained the same except that the countries played each other twice in the group stages.

And India won! Well, yes. On one hand, it was a surprise like no other that a 66-1 outsider won the game's greatest prize. But if you had followed their campaign, you would have noticed the sense of purpose to it. They defeated West Indies once in the group stage as well. They defeated Australia once in the group and England in the semis. Each member of the team contributed.

Roger Binny was the highest wicket-taker of the tournament. Madan Lal and Yashpal Sharma bowled their hearts out. Mohinder Amarnath chipped in with bat and ball to pick up Man of the Match awards in both the semis and the final.

And when Andy Roberts was the last wicket to fall, out LBW to Amarnath, there was mayhem all around. The spectators swarmed on to the field and people in India danced on the streets. Rahul Dravid remembers going out for an ice-cream with his family to celebrate. He felt that the entire country was out there with him.

It has been nearly twenty-eight years since that day. We are still waiting to dance on the streets again.

1987, INDIA AND PAKISTAN

What was the big deal? The Cup moved out of England for the first time. To Asia, which was fast becoming the hub of ODI cricket. India was the defending champion and Pakistan had a team that was among the best in the world.

What else? Once out of England, the long summer days were gone and the matches were of 50 overs each (instead of 60 in the first three editions).

So, Australia won. Yes, much to the dismay of the subcontinent crowd who hoped for either host to win. Australia came second in its group to face off with Pakistan in the semis and won with ease. The final against England was at Eden Gardens—the World Cup match with the highest attendance till date. England looked well on course to overhaul Australia's total of 253, when English captain Mike Gatting tried to reverse sweep Allan Border in a moment of madness and a collapse started. The fabled Aussie determination kicked in and they went on to clinch the match.

The captain-coach partnership of Allan Border and Bobby Simpson was the first of many successful duos that made Australia a world-beating side in another decade or so.

How did India do? After a one-run loss to Australia in the first match, India won five successive matches to set up a semi-final clash with England. In front of a vocal Bombay crowd, India allowed England to sweep the ground from under its feet and was ejected from the tournament.

1992, AUSTRALIA AND NEW ZEALAND

What was the big deal? A helluva lot. The first World Cup in Oceania had day-and-night matches, coloured clothing, white balls and black sight-screens—all for the first time.

What else? From the strategy point of view, there were a whole lot of innovations as well. Pinch-hitters were promoted by teams to take some quick runs at the beginning. Spinners opened the bowling to take advantage of helpful conditions. New laws governing rain interruptions came about, which very few people understood, least of all South Africa, whose target in the semi-final with England went from gettable to impossible due to a rain delay. Their departure was quite tragic since they were making a return to international cricket and had wowed everyone with their purposeful plays and spectacular fielding.

How did Pakistan win? That was the biggest surprise of the Cup. At one point, they had been bowled out for 74 by England when rain interrupted play and they avoided elimination. Using this one lifeline, Pakistan clawed back to reach the semis, where they beat an in-form New Zealand and then beat England in the final.

Led by the charismatic Imran Khan (who came out of retirement for this World Cup), Pakistan used the talent of its young guns—Wasim Akram and Inzamam Ul-Haq—as well as the passion and experience of its older stars to complete a Cup of dreams.

How did India do? Despite some hard fights, the Indian challenge fizzled out as it won only two out of eight group matches. The only consolation was that one of those wins came against the eventual champions and arch-rivals, Pakistan.

1996, INDIA, PAKISTAN, SRI LANKA

What was the big deal? Kaluwitharana c Tendulkar b Akram 6.

What? Yup, that's from the scorecard of a solidarity match played by a joint India-Pakistan team against Sri Lanka to show their confidence in the security arrangements of their co-host. This was after Australia and West Indies refused to play in Sri Lanka due to LTTE terror threats.

The ICC decided that games not played by any country against Sri Lanka would be awarded to the latter and thus, Sri Lanka became the first country to qualify for the quarter-final even before playing a match. With four out of six teams from each group qualifying for quarter-finals, Australia and West Indies still made it by defeating minnows like Kenya and Zimbabwe.

What are you saying, Sri Lanka won? Totally. They turned out to be the head-turner of the Cup. In Sanath Jayasuriya and Romesh Kaluwitharana, they had two T20 players who came a generation ahead. Blasting off during the field restrictions, they routinely scored 100+ runs in the first 15 overs. With strong batsmen to follow, captain Arjuna Ranatunga and coach Dav Whatmore built large totals with a batting powerhouse and defended them with emerging bowlers like Muttiah Muralitharan and Chaminda Vaas.

Against all odds, Sri Lanka beat all the biggies of world cricket to set up a title clash with Australia, and beat them fair and square to emerge as the newest kid on the block.

How did India do? India's shaky group performance—wins against Kenya, Zimbabwe and the West Indies and losses against Australia and Sri Lanka—was eclipsed by its rousing quarter-final victory against Pakistan. The semi-final was awarded to Sri Lanka when crowd trouble started after a batting collapse and did not allow the match to end.

1999, ENGLAND

What was the big deal? The Cup was back in the mother-ship but that was hardly something new. In hindsight, this World Cup signalled the beginning of Aussie domination of world cricket.

Which means, Australia won! Yes. More than the fact that it won, it was the way the team won. Despite being pushed to the wall (with group match defeats against New Zealand and Pakistan), it squeezed through to the Super Six, where it won all three matches.

In particular, the victory against South Africa has gone into cricketing lore for the way captain Steve Waugh forced a victory with a 110-ball 120. And when Herschelle Gibbs dropped his catch, Waugh played a high-stakes game of nerves by saying, 'You just dropped the World Cup, Hersh.'

The two teams met again in the semis and again, the Aussies held their nerves while the South Africans lost it. Needing just one off the last four balls, the last pair squandered it all and the match ended in a tie. The game was awarded to Australia because of its victory in the Super Six face-off. South Africa had indeed dropped the Cup.

With such momentum, Australia just decimated Pakistan in the final.

What else? The minnows started coming good. Bangladesh pulled off an upset victory against Pakistan. Zimbabwe defeated

India, South Africa and Kenya to reach the Super Six stage for the first time.

How did India do? In India's trademark patchy style, it lost to Zimbabwe in the group but managed to extract sweet revenge for the last World Cup with a towering win against Sri Lanka. Wins against Kenya and England took them to Super Six, where only a win against Pakistan was nowhere enough to take them to the semis.

2003, SOUTH AFRICA, ZIMBABWE AND KENYA

What was the big deal? The World Cup came to a country that had been ostracized from world cricket for nearly two decades. Coupled with the emergence of other African nations in world cricket, the Rainbow country was an apt venue for the game's biggest prize.

What else? Kenya made it to the semis.

What are you saying? Well, they were aided by a walkover from New Zealand, who refused to play in Nairobi but they still beat Sri Lanka, Zimbabwe (twice), Bangladesh and Canada. Obviously, the home advantage had some impact but there's no denying the exceptional quality of cricket played by Kenya in this World Cup.

Australia won again? Well, yes. They had an unbeaten run at the Cup, with no team even coming close to beating them.

Except for one match against England, which they won by 2 wickets, their lowest margin of victory was 48 runs or 5 wickets. Australia had truly overtaken Clive Lloyd's West Indies as the greatest cricket team of all times.

How did India do? Almost mind-blowing. India's best performance since 1983 came after a shaky start—an unsure win against Holland and being steamrolled by Australia. From then on, India played like a dream and beat Zimbabwe, Namibia, England, Pakistan, Kenya, Sri Lanka, New Zealand and again Kenya in the semis, to reach the final. There Australia blew India off. Sigh.

The captain-coach duo of Sourav Ganguly and John Wright had built a formidable team and this World Cup was a vindication of their partnership.

2007, WEST INDIES

What was the big deal? A lot of fans have always regarded cricket as a matter of life and death. With the death of Pakistani coach, Bob Woolmer, after a loss to first-timers Ireland, this proved gruesomely correct. The timing and the circumstances of the death were highly mysterious but the investigations could not conclusively prove any foul play. The incident cast a pall of gloom over the tournament.

What else? This World Cup could have been a complete vindication of the ICC policy of including associate nations into mainstream tournaments (after Kenya's performance in the previous edition).

Bangladesh and Ireland pulled off stunning upsets (against India and Pakistan respectively) and managed to reach the Super Eight stage. Unfortunately, the emergence of these teams could hardly be celebrated as allegations of match-fixing took centre stage immediately afterwards.

BTW, who won? Australia continued its juggernaut of clinical performances in all departments of the game. For the second successive World Cup, it had an undefeated run to complete a hat-trick of World Cup wins.

Interestingly, it had defeated an Asian team in each of the three finals.

How did India do? A disastrous outing. After the terrible loss to Bangladesh, India needed to win both its matches to make it to the next stage. After a record-breaking win against first-timers Bermuda, India lost to Sri Lanka to crash out at the group stage.

It was as if we were back in 1979. The only bright spot was that we all know what happened in 1983, don't we?

WORLD CUP SPONSORS

Very few sports in the world are as well suited for advertising as cricket. Each day's game has some hundred breaks between overs which can be filled with ads, not counting the longer breaks for drinks, lunch, tea and sometimes even strategizing.

For the first six World Cups, there was a title sponsor and the Cup was known by that name.

1975–83

Prudential Insurance Company, one of Britain's well-respected financial companies, sponsored the first three World Cups, all of which were known as Prudential Cup. When it entered India, Prudential was already known as the 'sponsor of the Cup India won'.

1987

When the Cup came to India, it was sponsored by the Reliance Group, then headed by Dhirubhai Ambani. The tournament was known as the Reliance Cup and it brought the fast-growing Reliance Group greater prominence in the Indian corporate scene.

Reliance Group has since been split into two groups, which are headed by Dhirubhai's sons, Mukesh and Anil. The elder son, Mukesh Ambani, is the owner of the IPL team, Mumbai Indians.

1992

Cigarette companies have always been big sponsors of cricketing tournaments. Benson & Hedges, a well-known tobacco brand, was the sponsor of the 1992 World Cup held in Australia and New Zealand. It had already been the sponsor of World Series Cricket Championships that were held since the early 1980s.

1996

It was the turn of yet another cigarette company, this time Indian, to sponsor the World Cup when it returned to India, Pakistan and Sri Lanka in 1996. ITC Limited was the sponsor of what was known as the Wills World Cup. For a period in

the 1990s, Wills was also the sponsor of the Indian cricket team.

With tougher laws against cigarette advertising that came in the late 1990s, these brands exited sports sponsorships.

1999 onwards, the scale of cricket had become massive and the title sponsorships involved amounts that were too large for one corporation to handle. Instead of one, ICC had several sponsors who were all associated with the World Cup. From then onwards, world cricket's biggest prize has just been known as the ICC World Cup.

11.

India at the World Cup: Ten Matches that Blew Our Minds

Indian cricketers have always defied logic. Some of their best performances have come as underdogs. They won two World Cups—ODI (1983) and T20 (2007)—when nobody expected them to. They also snatched defeat from the jaws of victory several times. A much-praised batting line-up has come to naught several times, unable to take the pressure.

Here is a list of the highs and lows that have happened at various World Cups, equally divided at five each. Some of them, true to Indian form, have come within days of each other. Most of them were causes of high emotion. All of them have contributed to the passion that characterizes Indian cricket.

1975, INDIA VS ENGLAND, LORD'S

Extremes always defy logic. Great innings leave us slack-jawed—how the hell did *that* happen? Monumentally bad plays have the same impact. More so, when the bad innings are played by one of the greatest batsman of modern age.

In a completely unfathomable day in the first ever cricket World Cup, Sunil Manohar Gavaskar scored 36 runs. In a 60-over match. While opening the innings. And remaining not out till the very end. Yes, rub your eyes and read the last bit once again.

Nobody really expected India to defeat England in the nineteenth ODI ever played. After all, England had scored a mammoth 334 runs batting first. But neither did anybody expect Gavaskar's innings. It is quite common in ODIs for struggling batsmen to start slogging and get out, so that other players can get the runs going. But nothing of that sort happened. Gavaskar plodded on and on till the overs ran out. One could say in his defence that India hardly had an ODI strategy at that time. But then, 60 overs are probably long enough to develop one!

England 334/4 in 60 overs (Dennis Amiss 137 in 147 balls) defeated India 132/3 in 60 overs (Sunil Gavaskar 36 in 174 balls).*

A quiz: Gavaskar faced 174 balls on that day. A boy, who was about two years old when this match was being played, faced 27 balls less in an ODI in February 2010. He scored 164 runs more. Know the boy?

1983, INDIA VS ZIMBABWE, TUNBRIDGE WELLS

BBC was on strike that day. It was in the middle of a World Cup but nobody really cared. After all, the two teams playing that day were not really in the contention for anything. By the fifth over of the day, India was 5 wickets down for 17 and even the Indian supporters started thinking that they were not really in contention for anything.

Except, a man called Kapil Dev was not out and not about to go down without a fight. As it turned out, he was not about to go down at all in that match!

175 runs is a great score, even in Tests. In ODIs, about a dozen people have overtaken it in the 27+ years between then and now. And nobody has done it after coming in to bat at such a precarious condition.

With only the bowlers Roger Binny, Ravi Shastri, Madan Lal and wicketkeeper Syed Kirmani for company, Kapil Dev played an innings of such savagery that the term 'captain's knock' would be woefully inadequate to describe it. 16 boundaries and 6 sixes were hammered as Kapil scored two-thirds of the team's runs. Such was his command over the match that the ninth-wicket partnership yielded 126 runs, of which he scored 102!

India went on to beat the best teams of the world in 1983 and lift the Cup. After this match, they probably started believing it was possible.

India 266/8 in 60 overs (Kapil Dev 175 in 138 balls) defeated Zimbabwe 235 in 57 overs (Kapil Dev 11-1-32-1).*

Kapil Dev, who usually batted at No. 6 or 7, never scored an ODI century again. His next best score was 87. But that's probably a good thing since a later order batsman scoring many runs means a top order collapse!

1983, INDIA VS WEST INDIES, LORD'S

One team was invited to the World Cup final of 1983. The other team gatecrashed. Not even the most hardcore fan expected India to win. The country was delirious to have made it this far and an honourable defeat at the hands of reigning world champions, West Indies, was considered acceptable.

And that's how the match played out in the beginning. Opener Krish Srikkanth's 38 turned out to be highest score of the innings and India did not even last the full quota of 60 overs, scoring a paltry 183.

Despite Balwinder Singh Sandhu getting opener Greenidge with a delivery that turned impossibly (after Greenidge left the delivery expecting it to go past), the hopes didn't rise. It couldn't have, with Vivian Richards hitting 7 boundaries to reach 33 in double quick time. And then the tide turned. Richard miscued a hit and the ball went high in the air. It did not look like a chance till Kapil Dev ran in from nowhere and took a catch that the entire country remembers.

The West Indian top order departed fast enough (76/6). Their bottom order steadied the ship a little bit but it just was not their day any longer. When Mohinder Amarnath got Michael Holding LBW, a sea of supporters invaded the ground in an unprecedented scene at the Home of Cricket.

And cricket became a religion in India.

India 183 (Srikkanth 38, Andy Roberts 10-3-32-3) defeated West Indies 140 (Viv Richards 33 in 28 balls, Madan Lal 12-2-31-3).

Sometimes, in the history of a country, comes an event so big that everyone can remember where they were at that very moment. This is called a Kennedy moment after the US President's shocking assassination.

For India, it is a happy one: 'What were you doing when Kapil lifted the Cup on 25 June 1983?' Interestingly, many Indian players in the 2011 World Cup team weren't even born! Captain M.S. Dhoni was two weeks short of two years old.

1987, INDIA VS ENGLAND, MUMBAI

India was the defending champion. India was playing on home turf. India was on a roll. The man who was infamous for his 36* crawl in 1975 had just scored a blistering century. The man who was hit for a last-ball-six by Javed Miandad had taken a hat-trick. India could do no wrong.

Except that the England batsmen had a clear plan, to which India had no answer. Graham Gooch and Mike Gatting had practised the sweep shot continuously in the nets. Despite knowing this,

Indian spinners bowled repeatedly on their legs, and the batsmen gleefully swept them for runs.

Despite facing a score that was buoyed by poor bowling, India managed to create some momentum in the chase but lost the plot towards the end.

With not many to get, Kapil Dev decided that he had to get them very fast. He tried to lift the ball over deep mid-wicket. The ball could not clear the ropes and the fielder, captain Mike Gatting, calmly swallowed the catch and with it, India's World Cup hopes.

India had been 'thought out' of the match.

England 254/6 in 50 overs (Graham Gooch 115, Mike Gatting 56) defeated India 219 in 45.3 overs (Azharuddin 64).

This match was played on 5 November 1987. Exactly twenty-two years later, Sachin Tendulkar scored 175 (in 141 balls) in a scintillating chase against Australia (who had scored 350) but India lost (by 3 runs). Is this date jinxed for India?

1996, INDIA VS PAKISTAN, BANGALORE

India and Pakistan seldom meet in a cricket match. It is always a war. And the World Cup is a battlefield that simply multiplies the stakes several times. Now, imagine that battlefield to be in the subcontinent. And the teams are facing off in a knock-out match—the quarter-finals of 1996.

The miracle man, Sachin Tendulkar, was surprisingly sedate in the match. He scored only 31 but Navjyot Sidhu scored 93 and the middle order contributed, too. Just when India was looking at a reasonably competitive total, in walked Ajay Jadeja and put the match in a different orbit. He took 40 off 2 Waqar Younis overs as the spectators went berserk and India reached a very impressive score of 287.

If Ajay Jadeja was brutal, Pakistani openers Aamer Sohail and Saeed Anwar were doubly so. They raced ahead at a run rate of 8+ and the match looked doomed for India. In a moment of overconfidence, Aamer Sohail hit Venkatesh Prasad for a four and made a cocky gesture. Prasad's anger led to a ripper in the next delivery that knocked the off-stump back. Prasad screamed back as the partisan crowd regained its voice as well. India clawed back into the match with wickets at regular intervals and Pakistan slumped to a 39-run loss.

As if the drama of the match was not enough, there was craziness after it as well. The Pakistani media accused India of devious conspiracies. One theory went that the Pakistanis were drugged in the innings break, which explained the collapse after an explosive start. Wasim Akram, who did not play the match due to an injury, was accused of treason.

The Indian media, on the other hand, proclaimed the team to be world beaters. But as it turned out, that was far from correct.

India 287/8 (Sidhu 93, Ajay Jadeja 45 in 25 balls) defeated Pakistan 248/9 (Aamer Sohail 55 in 46 balls, Saeed Anwar 48 in 32 balls).

1996, INDIA VS SRI LANKA, CALCUTTA

India walked into this match with the world at its feet and the World Cup two wins away. Sri Lanka was on a roll, but this was

where it was supposed to end. After all, Eden Gardens was Indian captain Mohammed Azharuddin's favourite hunting ground.

Azhar started with winning the toss. He put Sri Lanka in to bat, which did not seem like a good idea on a pitch that usually worsened in the evening. But all that was forgotten as both the Sri Lankan openers, Sanath Jayasuriya and Romesh Kaluwitharana, were dismissed in the very first over of the day. Their explosive batting had defeated India in an earlier group match, and getting them early seemed like a good omen. But Aravinda De Silva, playing the best cricket of his life, turned the game on its head. With incredible poise and aggression, he played a chanceless innings to get his team out of the woods.

Sachin Tendulkar started the chase easily enough and everything seemed to be on track. But nobody had really anticipated how bad the pitch could get and how much better Sachin was than the rest of the batsmen. After Sachin departed, India lost an incredible 6 wickets for 22 runs.

If the game was bad, the spectator behaviour was terrible. The Eden Gardens audience reacted violently and created a ruckus by throwing stones and bottles on the ground. After the police failed to restore order, the match was awarded to Sri Lanka in the only such instance of World Cup history.

And the abiding memory of India's 1996 World Cup campaign was the sight of Vinod Kambli walking off the pitch, in tears.

Sri Lanka 251/8 (Aravinda De Silva 66 in 47 balls, Roshan Mahanama 58) awarded match against India 120/8 (Sachin Tendulkar 65, Sanath Jayasuriya 7-1-12-3)

1999, INDIA VS SRI LANKA, TAUNTON

In the years after the last World Cup, India saw the emergence of two batting stars, who quickly went on to become the mainstay of Indian batting. Rahul Dravid and Sourav Ganguly both made their remarkable debuts in the same Test in England and when the World Cup returned to England in 1999, their contributions were expected to be high.

When India met Sri Lanka for a group match, they had never beaten the Emerald Islanders in a World Cup, with the last face-off ending in an Indian disaster. They lost a wicket in the first over of the day, to make matters worse. Then, Dravid came in to join Ganguly and the match was a different ball game altogether. The duo batted for 45 overs and put on an incredible 318 runs, breaking or nearing pretty much every ODI batting record of the time.

The onslaught was so comprehensive and the target (374 to win) so formidable that Sri Lanka collapsed in a heap early in the chase. Last World Cup's hero, Aravinda De Silva, top scored but they never even came close to becoming a threat. All-rounder Robin Singh took 5 wickets.

The Ganguly-Dravid duo went on to greater heights as batsmen (twenty-one century partnerships in Tests and ODIs) as well as leaders of Indian cricket. Their stint as captain and vice-captain of India is one of the best periods of the team's history. This match was a preview.

India 373/6 in 50 overs (Ganguly 183 in 158 balls, Dravid 145 in 129 balls) defeated Sri Lanka 216 in 42.3 overs (Aravinda De Silva 56, Robin Singh 9.3-0-31-5).

2003, INDIA VS PAKISTAN, CENTURION

India, despite having a poor overall record against Pakistan is undefeated against them in the World Cups. When they met in the 2003 World Cup in South Africa, this record was boosted by the fact that India was on a roll and no team other than Australia looked anywhere near it. But with bowlers like Shoaib Akhtar and Wasim Akram, a match-winning performance could just be one over away.

Batting first, Pakistan rode on a classy century from opener Saeed Anwar, who was dependable as always. Their middle-order contributed as well and they reached a score (273) that is always a tricky one to chase.

When Tendulkar and Sehwag walked in to bat, the pressure was squarely on India. After all, Pakistan knew that the Indian batting tended to fold up alarmingly fast if Tendulkar departed early.

That got settled pretty fast. The first few overs were pure mayhem. Sehwag thumped 9 off the first over from Wasim Akram. Sachin doubled that effort and slammed the second over, Shoaib Akhtar's, for 18. Playing with merciless abandon, the duo used the speed of the Pakistan pace attack to cross the boundary ropes almost at will. When Sachin got out for 98 (off 75 balls, including a dozen fours and a six off Shoaib), the match was almost in the pocket. In fact, the initial momentum was strong enough for Dravid and Yuvraj to settle down and see India to a convincing win (with 4.2 overs to spare).

Cricket is always believed to be a team game. But in matches like these, that belief gets challenged. And it takes a performer like Sachin Tendulkar to do that.

Pakistan (273/7 in 50 overs, Saeed Anwar 101, Zaheer Khan 10-0-46-2) lost to India (276/4 in 45.4 overs, Tendulkar 98 in 75 balls, Yuvraj 50, Dravid 44*)*

2003, INDIA VS AUSTRALIA, JOHANNESBURG

In the 2003 World Cup, only one team looked capable of beating India. And India met that team in the finals.

As the match was about to start, none of the experts seriously gave India a chance. Except for an astrologer who claimed that the Indian skipper, Sourav Ganguly, had a very good time coming up that evening.

When Australia came in to bat, they unleashed an assault that proved all the experts right and broke the hearts of Indian fans. First the openers and then captain Ricky Ponting took apart the Indian pacers, who were expected to get some assistance from the Wanderers pitch by bowling first. Ponting scored an unbeaten century and took Australia to a mammoth score (359).

In the fifth ball of the Indian over, Glenn McGrath caught, off his own bowling, Sachin Tendulkar, and won the match for Australia.

Nothing that happened afterwards—Sehwag scoring a brilliant 82, Ganguly and Sehwag taking 19 off a McGrath over, Dravid scoring a useful 47—could change the sense of the inevitable that sets in after Sachin Tendulkar gets out in the first over of a 360-run chase.

Oh yes, the astrologer's prediction threatened to come true as it started raining quite heavily around the seventeenth over of India's batting and an abandoned match meant replaying it the next day. Unfortunately, for India and the astrologer, the rain was not heavy enough to bring about Ganguly's hour of glory. India crashed to a 125-run loss.

Australia 359/2 (Ricky Ponting 140 in 121 balls, Damien Martyn 88 in 84 balls, Adam Gilchrist 57 in 48 balls) defeated India 234 in 39.2 overs (Sehwag 82 in 81 balls, Dravid 47).

2007, INDIA VS BANGLADESH, TRINIDAD

In the preliminary rounds of every World Cup, some minnows are always grouped with the top-ranked teams so that the big guys get some match practice and can break some records before moving into the later rounds. Bangladesh, though improving greatly under Dav Whatmore, who was Sri Lanka's coach when they won the 1996 World Cup, was supposed to sweat India a bit but not do much damage in the opening match of India's 2007 World Cup campaign.

Halfway into the Indian batting, India was gasping for breath as almost the entire top order had departed (72/4 that included Sehwag, Uthappa, Tendulkar, Dravid). Sourav Ganguly, who was back from the wilderness after a long layoff from the Indian team, put up a brief resistance but the rest of the team collapsed around him and 5 wickets fell between 157 and 159 runs.

Bangladesh, when it came in to bat, played like men possessed. It looked to be in sniffing distance of pulling off one of the biggest upsets in World Cup history and weren't about to let go. Eventually, the minnows did manage to pull off exactly what nobody expected them to.

India 191 in 49.3 overs (Sourav Ganguly 66, Yuvraj Singh 47) lost to Bangladesh 192/5 in 48.3 overs (Mushfiqur Rahim 56, Shakib Al Hasan 53, Tamim Iqbal 51).

Coach Greg Chappell, already under fire for his controversial methods, was blamed for not being able to raise the team's performance and quit soon after the debacle. Indian fans reacted in their usual illogical manner of attacking players' homes and burning effigies.

However, the good news was that all was forgiven immediately afterwards as India went on to defeat Bangladesh in Tests and ODIs and had good matches against South Africa and England.

That's how we follow cricket in India. It is either a level of worship where millions line the roads as our heroes do a victory procession in open-top buses. Or we stone our captain's home and put his family to grievous harm while he is still in transit after a bad tournament.

Love. Passion. Emotion.

Cricket strategy—what's that?

12.

No Hope Victories

The ultimate high in a cricket match is when you win after giving up all hope. Wickets are tumbling or the opposition batting is on a roll. You switch off the TV and start preparing for the Maths test.

But there is a hubbub. A bubbling of spectator emotion. You are now curious. Who are they still cheering? And why? Could they possibly have ... You rush to switch the TV back on. And are just in time to catch the final two overs, in which another unbelievable victory is sealed.

If there was a heaven on earth, it is here, it is here, it is here...

1985, INDIA VS PAKISTAN, SHARJAH

Facing off in the desert stadium of Sharjah, India was put into bat and they immediately ran into a hurricane called Imran Khan, who claimed opener Ravi Shastri in the first ball of the day. In a longish first spell, he sent back Srikkanth, Gavaskar, Vengsarkar and Amarnath after that. At 34/5, captain Kapil Dev joined Mohammed Azharuddin, an exciting new batsman who had had a brilliant debut the previous year. The two of them did a bit of repair work, but 125 runs were all they could get to. Imran Khan finished with one of the best ODI bowling figures, having taken 6 wickets for a mere 14 runs.

This was the point people switched off. 125 was going to get knocked off in a hurry by Miandad & Co.

Pakistan started strongly enough and reached 35/1. Then, a strange thing happened. They lost 4 wickets for 6 runs, to three different bowlers. At 41/5, Rameez Raja (now a well-known commentator) started to consolidate. After all, only 80-odd runs were needed and he got 33 runs before he lost his partner. With the score at 85, captain Kapil Dev got Rameez and the balance 3 wickets in a span of 2 runs.

India had completed a totally stunning victory through a complete team effort. Kapil got 3 wickets, Sivaramakrishnan and Shastri got two each, Binny and Madan Lal 1 each while Gavaskar pouched 4 catches.

India's record at Sharjah was very poor but at least the beginning was auspicious.

India 125 all out in 42.4 overs (Azharuddin 47, Kapil Dev 30) defeated Pakistan 87 all out in 32.5 overs (Rameez Raja 29).

1996, INDIA VS AUSTRALIA, BANGALORE

Australia batted first. And despite two early wickets, captain Mark Taylor and fighter Steve Waugh steadied the ship with a 92-run partnership. Michael Bevan came in to do a great job of scoring quick runs in the end overs and the Aussies ended up at a competitive-but-gettable 215. Bangalore lustily cheered its local boys Javagal Srinath (10-2-35-0) and Anil Kumble (10-0-40-2), who did their bit of containing and getting wickets.

Of course, India immediately made heavy weather of the chase. They lost opener Somasunder, Dravid, captain Azharuddin and Ganguly by 47. Sachin, as always, hung in and tried building partnerships. Ajay Jadeja and Nayan Mongia were useful people to have in the lower order, but India's hopes were pinned on Sachin taking it to the very end.

With the score at 164, Sachin was the eighth batsman to fall and Anil Kumble walked in to join Srinath.

This was the point where India either switched off TVs or went off to have dinner. You don't really expect two tail-enders to get 52 runs at about run-a-ball. Not against Australia, at least.

The two underdogs quietly started their rescue act.

Rescue acts of this magnitude never happen quietly. As Srinath upped the scoring rate and Kumble pushed the scores along, the stadium erupted. The fever spread across the nation and TV sets got switched back on. Their home crowd went crazy as they took India to victory with 7 balls to spare.

You may forget how Srinath bowled or how many wickets Kumble took in his career, but if you watched *this* match, you will never forget how they batted!

Australia 215/7 (Mark Taylor 105, Steve Waugh 44, Michael Bevan 36) lost to India 216/8 in 48.5 overs (Sachin Tendulkar 88, Srinath 30 in 23 balls, Kumble 16 in 19 balls).

2002, INDIA VS ENGLAND, LORD'S

The Indian team under Sourav Ganguly was a new one and shaping quite well, but they seemed to be losing all the finals. To shake off the label of 'chokers', this team had to win this final of the NatWest Trophy at the end of a hard-fought English season.

It started off like a nightmare. After winning the toss, English captain Nasser Hussain chose to bat and promptly justified the decision with a 185-run partnership with Marcus Trescothick. With plenty of wickets and overs in hand, England tried to force the pace but lost a couple of wickets. Despite that, they reached a formidable total of 325 runs.

The bad news was that nobody had successfully chased 326 till then. The best effort was only 316. The good news was that it was India who did that as well!

The Indian reply started explosively enough. Sehwag and Ganguly tore into the English attack and when the latter got out, India had reached 106 in the first 15 overs. Then, the collapse started. Sehwag left in the very next over. 3 more wickets fell within the next 30 runs including that of Sachin Tendulkar.

When Sachin leaves less than halfway through a 300+ run chase, you don't hang around to see the potential of two greenhorns. Yuvraj Singh and Mohammed Kaif could well have been the future of Indian cricket but they weren't considered good enough to keep the TVs on.

Except that, they were.

They put together a 121-run partnership for the sixth wicket and when Yuvraj got out at 267, a glimmer of hope was seen. Of course, their batting had brought back the cheers and the viewers. Some late jitters happened as Harbhajan swung his bat and left, Kumble left without scoring and Zaheer Khan came in at No. 10. However, Kaif was the man on a mission who steered India to an incredible victory with 3 balls to spare.

And we got to see the most defining image of Sourav Ganguly taking off his shirt and twirling it in the air (in a reply to Flintoff, who did the same in an earlier series)—an apt symbol of the New India, who celebrated wildly but after stunning wins!

England 325/5 (Nasser Hussain 115, M. Trescothick 109) lost to India 326/8 in 49.3 overs (Mohammed Kaif 87, Yuvraj Singh 69, Ganguly 60).*

Indian cricket is all about hope. And surprises—pleasant ones and some not-so-pleasant ones. As an ad for a soft drink once said, we never know who will pull off a famous victory. Even Kumble and Srinath can bat us to a win. That's our strategy. Who's the batsman? Who's the bowler? We don't know till the last ball is bowled!

13.

Talking Cricket: Cricket Commentary Down the Ages

The first ever cricket commentary happened in 1922, for a match being played at the Sydney Cricket Ground. It was only in 1938 that radio commentary became really popular. It happened with something called a 'synthetic broadcast' (again, in Australia).

In this system, the commentator usually sat in a studio far away from the match. He was provided with the match details at the end of every over, and he repeated it in present tense, as if he was reporting live. Sometimes, stadium sound effects were recreated by tapping tables with pencils (bat on ball) and using recorded crowd reactions!

As the portable transistor radio became popular in India, so did the practice of following cricket on it. All India Radio had a battery of commentators who spoke in Hindi and English and reported the games in intricate and poetic detail in their sonorous voices. When overseas tours started, Indian fans set alarms and woke up at unearthly hours (10 a.m. in Australia means 5 a.m. in India!) to catch the commentary.

A familiar sight outside newspaper offices (till about the 1960s) would be a large blackboard where the scores would be updated every fifteen minutes. This device was borrowed from the elections where results of seats would be similarly announced. Dictionaries, and even current affairs magazines, carried diagrams of cricket fields showing the field placements. Newbies had to keep one open in front of them to get the hang of 'deep mid-wicket' and 'short fine leg'.

The first ever cricket telecast happened way back in 1938, at Lord's in London. But the quality and quantity of television broadcast remained minuscule for the next three decades.

Television in India started in the 1970s and the following of cricket reached a new level. This was also the decade when World Series Cricket started in Australia and cricket broadcasting became even more fun.

In 1985, India played—and won—the Benson & Hedges World Championship in Australia. That's when the Indian and subcontinent audience saw the broadcasting style of Channel 9, that had added several dimensions to cricket coverage. Multi-camera set-ups became popular across the globe as every run-out, every missed catch and every LBW appeal was dissected from all possible angles. As if stump cameras were not enough to see the ball zipping in and crashing into the screen, there were stump mikes as well. If the players said something naughty on the field, there was no way they wouldn't get caught!

With such high-tech coverage, umpiring mistakes became much easier to catch and very soon, a clamour to use technology for umpiring decisions started. In 1992-'93, the concept of the third umpire started who sat in a TV room to decide on run-out and stumping appeals.

Like many other firsts to his name, Sachin Tendulkar also became the first ever batsman to be given out on a TV replay. This happened in a match against South Africa. Quite fittingly, the fielder was Jonty Rhodes, probably the greatest fielder ever.

As the viewing technology boomed, so did the analysis. Cool graphics became a part of watching cricket and words like Manhattan, Wagon Wheel, Hawk Eye, Snicko entered our vocabulary.

***Manhattan**–the graph showing the runs scored in every over, so called because it looks like the skyscrapers of downtown New York.*

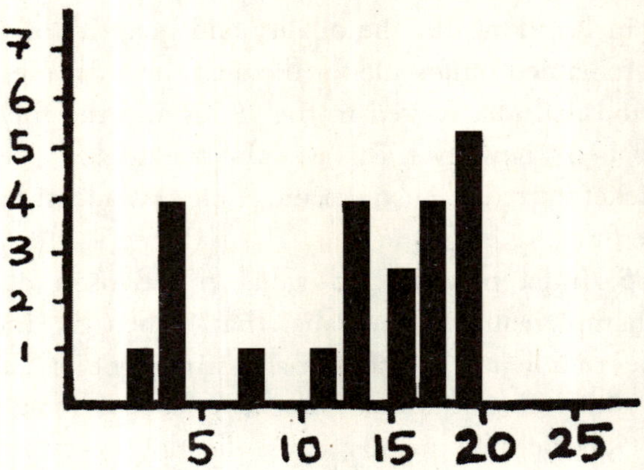

***Wagon Wheel**–the runs scored by a batsman across the ground, so called because all the lines look like spokes of a wheel.*

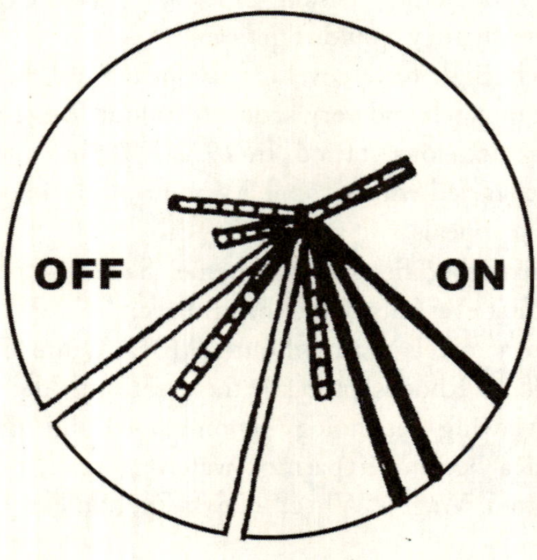

Hawk Eye*–the computer simulation of a cricket ball's path when it hits the pads to see if it would have gone on to hit the stumps.*

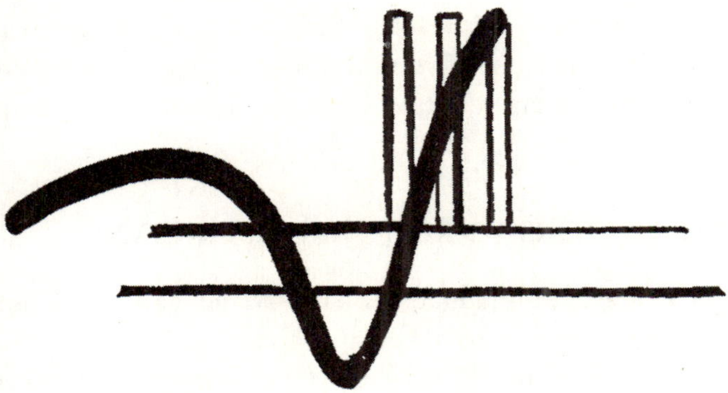

Snickometer*–output from the stump microphone to see if there was a noise when the ball went past the bat that indicates a touch.*

As television brought a massive audience to the game, its power also changed the way the game was played. Nowadays, playing time is decided on the basis of prime-time TV timings. Day-and-night cricket started almost only because the exciting end-overs happened when TV viewership was at its peak.

From television, cricket viewing has moved on to the next medium—Internet and mobile.

Online ball-by-ball commentaries are quite common and fun because the commentary teams take in questions and opinions from surfers and put them up on the site, as if you are watching the match with friends.

Cricket on mobile started off with SMSing 'CRI' to a service provider and receiving a message with the latest cricket score. It has since then moved on to having mobile applications that are downloaded on the phone and keep refreshing automatically.

With IPL 3 (in 2010), YouTube started broadcasting live cricket matches and mobiles with 3G connections can also do the same. The game is still bursting out of screens. Only the sizes and numbers seem to have changed.

With all the technology, it was long feared that spectators would abandon the stadium. Thankfully, that fear has turned out to be unfounded as thousands still throng to watch live cricket. No technology can beat the feeling of dancing in the stands when a six lands a little in front of you. And it helps that stadium screens now show replays and electronic scoreboards catch pretty much every stat!

COMMENTATORS TO KEEP AN EAR OUT FOR

Harsha Bhogle: A graduate of IIM-A, he gave up a job in an advertising agency to take up a full-time career in cricket commentary. From the 1992 World Cup onwards, he has been a knowledgeable and enthusiastic presence, known for his cheerful, chatty commentary style.

Navjyot Singh Sidhu: This Indian opener never seemed to be very articulate in his playing days. But he burst on to the commentary scene with multi-coloured turbans, a shrill voice and a never-ending series of silly phrases (now known as Sidhuisms). A regular at TV comedy shows, he is most likely to say, 'Indian batting is like a cycle stand. If one falls, it takes the rest of them with it.'

Sunil Gavaskar: When he retired from international cricket as the world's highest run-getter, he already had a formidable reputation as an author and columnist. He has added to that by being a very balanced commentator who not only has a keen knowledge of the game but a stern word of advice for budding cricketers as well.

Ravi Shastri: After a premature end to his career as all-rounder, due to injuries, he hit the commentary circuit with a mix of knowledge and on-air showmanship. While his knowledge of the game is never in question, repeated use of his pet phrases is a common complaint against him. Wait for him to say 'that's what the doctor ordered' or 'that will set the cat among the pigeons'!

Geoff Boycott: Not as popular now as he was a few years back, this English opener made his name by being the plain-speaker among the commentators. His a style was distinctive because of his Yorkshire accent ('roobish' instead of 'rubbish') and harsh pronouncements ('Even my grandmother could have caught that').

THE LONG AND SHORT

If commentators had to take the full names of bowlers when they ran in to bowl, lunch would have been called by the time they got Warnakulasuriya Patabendige Ushantha Joseph Chaminda Vaas (fifty-two letters) correctly. Phew!

Interestingly, he is not an exception in the Sri Lankan team. Ace batsman Denagamage Proboth Mahela de Silva Jayawardene (forty-one letters) is not far behind as is not-so-regular medium-pacer Uda Walawwe Mahim Bandaralage Chanaka Asanga Welegedara (forty-nine letters). In fact, Sri Lanka has a near-monopoly on the longest names in international cricket. Actually, when you see initials like KMDN Kulasekara, BAW Mendis and NLTC Perera on the scorecard, you start to wonder where their usual names are hiding!

On the other hand, Imran Khan is a breeze. At nine letters, it could well be the shortest full name among international cricketers (though all profiles of his contain Niazi as a last name, taking him up to fourteen letters).

In the current crop of Indian players, Irfan and Yusuf Pathan both weigh in at eleven letters each—except that their full names have a Khan in the middle.

Therefore, the shortest full names in the squad would be Zaheer Khan, Virat Kohli or Amit Mishra (ten letters each). Any shorter than that and it won't be a full name to start with!

Full names of Indian cricketers can be tricky, too. Many Indian cultures don't have a concept of a middle name. Maharashtrians, on the other hand, insert the father's name to make the name 'full'. Therefore, Sachin Ramesh Tendulkar is the correct full name (twenty-one letters, in case you are wondering) but Sourav Chandidas Ganguly is not!

In fact, Sourav Ganguly is a thirteen-letter delicacy—not unlike his cover drives—unless he decides to use the exact transliteration of the original Bengali version of his surname. In that case, his name expands by 39 per cent to Sourav Gangopadhyay.

Interestingly, the Indian cricket team is full of surnames that are the only ones to have made it. For example, there is only one of Gavaskar, Vengsarkar, Sehwag and Dhoni. Why, we have only one Tendulkar who made it to the national team even though it is quite a common Marathi surname.

The most common surname of Indian nationals would be Singh or Khan, with large numbers of both. But it is good to have heroes with nearly-unique names. Sherlock Holmes wouldn't have been half as interesting if he had been David Holmes. Virender Sehwag has a swagger about the name which Virender Trivedi doesn't. After all, the name has to be as striking as the shots!

And if you want striking names, the last word has to be with the teenager who is part of the Chennai Super Kings and Tamil Nadu squad. We should desperately pray that he comes good and the India team will have a general and a genius—Napoleon Einstein!

PART B

The Cup Quest

1.

India: The Men in Blue

No team in any sport in any part of the world has a billion people rooting for it! No single sport unifies an entire country like cricket unites India. And never are the prayers so fervent as they are every four years, when the Men in Blue gun for the biggest prize in cricket.

Fifteen men have been chosen to bear the burden of these billion hopes. They are are not only exceptional cricketers but extremely brave warriors as well. They accept our good wishes with humility. They bear our anger with patience. And whatever be the result and whatever we may say in moments of anger, they are people who give their all on the cricket pitch.

Some members of the team have debuted at around eighteen years of age, about the time many of us take our Class XII exams.

Many held world records by the time they were twenty-four years old, about the time people start their first jobs. At a time when normal people are still studying or looking for jobs, these youngsters go around conquering the world.

If you see their debuts, you will find an astounding majority of them failing miserably. And yet they have come back. Despite all odds, poor form, injuries, they have come back to the top.

Here are quick profiles of some of the men who will carry India's hopes in the World Cup.

Many of them are yet to play in a World Cup. Here's hoping that all of them and their coach would have won one by March!

Name / Nickname
Mahendra Singh Dhoni / Mahi

Date of birth
7 July 1981

Teams
Jharkhand, Chennai Super Kings (captain)

ODI Debut
Against Bangladesh in December 2004.
Got run-out for a first ball duck!

Averages
India's captain has a batting average of 50+, which is third highest in the world among batsmen who have played more than 100 ODI innings. And these runs have come at a fast pace (strike rate nearly 90), making MSD one of the most feared batsmen in the world.
As a wicketkeeper, he keeps a cool head behind the stumps and is not seen losing his cool during matches.

World Cup Performance
2007.
29 runs in 3 matches. 5 catches, 2 stumpings.

Most memorable performance
Came into the limelight with a 148 (in 123 balls) that he made after coming one down as a rank newcomer. His long hair, cool style and hard hitting made him an instant hit with fans.

Trivia
Currently enrolled in St Xavier's College, Ranchi for a Bachelor's degree in Business Management and Secretarial Practice. He got admission under the sports quota and is exempt from attending classes. Highest paid sportsperson from India. Recently signed a Rs 210 crore three-year endorsement deal, beating Sachin Tendulkar's deal to be the highest ever.

Name / Nickname
Virender Sehwag / Viru

Date of birth
20 October 1978

Teams
Delhi, Delhi Daredevils

ODI Debut
Against Pakistan in April 1999. Came in at No. 7 and scored 1 (in 2 balls).

Averages
That Sehwag has a strike rate of 100+ should not surprise anyone. The surprise is that his ODI record is not as good as his Test record and his batting average is only around 35. But the fear he induces in bowlers across the world is something else!
An useful off-spinner, he has nearly 100 ODI wickets and manages to churn out a few overs in the fifth bowler's quota.

World Cup Performance
2003 and 2007 World Cups.
2003: 299 runs in 11 innings. Highest 82 in the final against Australia. SR 87.
2007: 164 runs in 3 innings. Highest 114 against Bermuda. SR 118.

Most memorable performance
Innumerable. A man with two triple-centuries and a Test strike rate of 81 is obviously a man of magic.
But the most memorable moment is probably when he got out at 195 (against Australia), trying to hit a six.

Trivia
Sehwag loves reaching milestones with sixes. When he was batting with Sachin Tendulkar in Multan, Sachin asked him to be cautious and threatened him 'If you try to hit a six, I will hit you on the bum.' But when Sehwag was on 295, he ignored Sachin and hit a six to reach his triple-century.
Apart from endorsing commercial products, Sehwag is also a brand ambassador for

Delhi Police asking people to drive safely and to respect women.

Name / Nickname
Gautam Gambhir / Gauti

Date of birth
14 October 1981

Teams
Delhi, Delhi Daredevils (captain in IPL 3)

ODI Debut
Against Bangladesh in April 2003. Opened the innings and scored 11 in 22 balls.

Averages
India's Test opener comes at No. 3 in ODIs and is a stable run-gatherer. His strike rate (around 85) shows that he does not waste too much time at the crease and his average (hovering under 40) shows he gets a few runs on board as well.

World Cup Performance
Yet to play in a World Cup.

Most memorable performance
Key player in India's winning performance at the 2007 ICC World T20, where he scored a rocking 75 off 54 balls in the final against Pakistan.
After a very consistent batting performance (2008 onwards) that included 8 centuries from 13 Tests, Virender Sehwag called him the 'best Indian Test opener since Sunil Gavaskar'.

Trivia
Though a very controlled batsman, Gambhir has had two infamous run-ins on the pitch. One was when he was suspended for throwing an elbow at Shane Watson and the other was a verbal duel with Shahid Afridi, when he went eyeball-to-eyeball after a mid-pitch collision.

Name / Nickname
Harbhajan Singh / Bhajji / The Turbanator

Date of birth
3 July 1980

Teams
Mumbai Indians, Lancashire, Surrey

ODI Debut
Against New Zealand in April 1998. Bowled 10 overs for an economical 32 runs and took 1 wicket.

Averages
In the current team, Harbhajan is India's leading wicket-taker and strike bowler. At an economy rate of just more than 4 runs per over and an average of around 30, he is India's big hope in the middle overs. He is also a handy batsman to have in the team, capable of pushing up the scoring rate in the later overs. His top ODI innings have all come at a strike rate of nearly 150!

World Cup Performance
2003 and 2007 World Cups.
2003: 11 wickets in 9 innings. Maintained economy rates of around 4 for all matches except two against Australia!
2007: 0 wickets for 83 runs in 2 innings against Bangladesh and Sri Lanka, both of which India lost.

Most memorable performance
Usually reserves his best against Australia. In the turnaround Test series of 2001, Harbhajan took an amazing 32 wickets, while the next highest Indian wicket-taker took 3, and sealed his place in the team.
Has often chipped in with explosive batting performances. In the 2010 Asia Cup, he scored a penultimate-ball six against Pakistan to take India to victory.

Trivia
A fun-loving guy, he partnered with TV actress Mona Singh

to win a TV dance competition called *Ek Khiladi Ek Haseena* (in which cricketers were paired with actresses).
Harbhajan's two worst run-ins were with Sreesanth (whom he slapped after an IPL match) and Andrew Symonds (who accused him of calling him a 'monkey'—a racial abuse—but later emerged that it was a similar-sounding Punjabi *gaali*)!

Name / Nickname
Yuvraj Singh / Yuvi

Date of birth
12 December 1981

Teams
Punjab, Kings XI Punjab, Yorkshire

ODI Debut
Against Kenya in October 2000. Did not bat. Bowled 4 overs and gave away 16 runs. Exploded in the very next match against Australia. 84 runs in a victory nobody expected!

Averages
Though he has been in and out of the team in recent times due to a weight problem and poor form, Yuvraj Singh's talent is undeniable. Despite coming in at No. 5/6, he has 12 centuries and 43 fifties in ODIs.

As a left-arm bowler, he can be depended on to push in a few overs in the middle of the innings also.

World Cup Performance
2003 and 2007 World Cups.
2003: 240 runs in 10 innings (Average 34, SR 85). Scored a patient 50 to ensure victory against Pakistan.
2007: 136 runs in 3 innings (Average 45, SR 117), of which 83 (off 46 balls) came against Bermuda.

Most memorable performance
Natwest Trophy final, where he (69 off 63 balls) and Mohammed Kaif took India to 326 runs after a batting collapse.
Hit Stuart Broad for six sixes in a T20 over en route to winning the ICC World T20.

Trivia
For his six sixes and great all-round performance at the ICC World T20, Yuvraj was gifted a Porsche 911 by BCCI.

Name / Nickname
Virat Kohli

Date of birth
5 November 1988

Teams
Delhi, Royal Challengers Bangalore

ODI Debut
Against Sri Lanka in August 2008. Opened the batting and scored 12 runs in 22 balls in a total score of 146. India lost by 8 wickets!

Averages
Has a 46+ batting average in ODIs, which have come at a rapid pace (strike rate of 80+). He is a handy middle-order batsman who relishes chasing big totals. In fact, he averages 60+ while batting second, which is double his average while batting first.

The last couple of years have been very good for Kohli. He has been among the top ten batting averages in the world (since January 2009), behind only Sachin and Dhoni.

World Cup Performance
Yet to play in a World Cup.

Most memorable performance
Against Australia in 2010, Kohli played a brilliant knock of 118 (in only 121 balls). This came while chasing a massive 290 and he came in when the first wicket had fallen at zero. He had two solid partnerships with Yuvraj Singh and Suresh Raina.

Trivia
Virat Kohli was the captain of the Under-19 World Cup winning team in Malaysia, 2008.

In 2006, he lost his father in the middle of a Ranji match against Karnataka and still returned to bat the next day, managing to avoid a follow-on for his team (Delhi).

Name / Nickname
Yusuf Pathan

Date of birth
17 November 1982

Teams
Baroda, Rajasthan Royals

ODI Debut
Against Pakistan in June 2008. Came in as a pinch-hitter at No. 4 and scored 3 in 12 balls. Bowled 2 overs for 11 runs.

Averages
In his short ODI career, Yusuf has a strike rate of 100+ and has managed to hit a flurry of sixes whenever he has settled in. His batting average is still poor (20s) and is occasionally suspect against pace bowling. But on Indian pitches, he is a batsman no bowler likes to bowl to!

World Cup Performance
Yet to play in a World Cup.

Most memorable performance
Yusuf Pathan has had a series of explosive performances in the Indian Premier League, including the fastest century of the tournament. Scored against Mumbai Indians, Pathan scored 100 runs in 37 balls. The sequence of runs was an unbelievable 1.1.1.2.1. 6.0.0.0.1.1.1.0.0.6.6.6.6.4.4.6. 4.4.4.4.1.0.4.1.1.2.4.1.1.6.4.6 And after all this, his team lost!

Trivia

Older brother of Irfan Pathan, Yusuf Pathan, debuted four years after him.

Name / Nickname

Suresh Raina

Date of birth

27 November 1986

Teams

Uttar Pradesh, Chennai Super Kings

ODI Debut

Against Sri Lanka in July 2005. Scored a 'golden duck' (out first ball), out LBW to Muralitharan!
Bowled the last over and was hit by Jayasuriya for a winning four off the second delivery.

Averages

One of India's youngest stars, Raina is an ODI specialist who played 98 ODIs before his Test debut! Known for his ability to clear the field with his lofted shots, Raina has a solid strike rate (nearly 90) and a decent average (around 35).
An athletic fielder at point, Raina is the man to have in the team.

World Cup Performance

Yet to play in a World Cup.

Most memorable performance

In the 2008 Asia Cup, he was Man of the Match for three successive matches. Two of them were for centuries against Hong Kong and Bangladesh.
In the match against Pakistan, he scored 84 off 69 balls and put on 198 runs in less than 25 overs (in partnership with Sehwag) to chase down 300 runs in only 42 overs!

Trivia

His Test debut came five years after his ODI debut and Suresh Raina became the twelfth Indian to score a century on debut.

Name / Nickname
Zaheer Khan / Zak

Date of birth
7 October 1978

Teams
India, Baroda, Mumbai, Mumbai Indians, Surrey, Worcestershire

ODI Debut
Against Kenya in October 2000.
Took 3 wickets in his quota of 10 overs, giving away 48 runs.

Averages
One of the best fast bowlers India has produced, Zaheer can do reverse swing, yorkers and bouncers. With nearly 250 wickets, he is India's most experienced fast bowler and is known to bowl tight (economy rate of less than 5). He is the man to get India the early breakthroughs.

World Cup Performance
2003 and 2007 World Cups.
2003: 18 wickets in 11 innings (India's highest wicket-taker). Maintained economy rates of around 4 in the tournament despite going for 67 runs in 7 overs in the final against Australia!
2007: 5 wickets for 122 runs in 3 innings (29 overs). Just not enough, despite an impressive economy rate (just above 4).

Most memorable performance
Best bowling against Sri Lanka, when he got 5 wickets for only 42 runs in 10 overs. In an inspired burst of pace bowling, he removed three batsmen in his first two overs.

Trivia
Zaheer holds a batting record. His score of 75 against Bangladesh in 2004 is the highest score by a last man in Test cricket. He put on 133 runs for the last wicket with Sachin Tendulkar.

Name / Nickname
Gary Kirsten

Date of birth
23 November 1967

Teams
South Africa

ODI Debut
Against Australia in December 1993.
Scored 4 runs, spending 27 balls in the process (and his team collapsed for only 69)!

Averages
Has nearly 7,000 runs at an average of 40+, which has been scored at a decent strike rate. With 13 hundreds, Gary Kirsten was one of the most dependable opening batsmen in the formidable South African team of the 1990s. Thanks to his stellar record, he is greatly respected in the Indian team.

World Cup Performance
Has played in three World Cups—1996, 1999 and 2003—making him the second-most experienced World Cupper in the team!

Has scored 806 runs in all, at an average of 47.

Most memorable performance
In the 1996 World Cup, he scored an amazing 188 (off only 159 balls) against minnows UAE, which was one run short of the highest ODI innings at that time (Viv Richards' 189*).

Trivia
Gary Kirsten runs a company called Performance Zone with Paddy Upton, the mental conditioning coach of India. The company helps teams and companies improve their performances.

2.

Sachin Tendulkar

In November 1989, a two-year-old-boy called Lionel Messi was probably being toilet trained in a small town called Rosario in Argentina.

It was also the year Boris Becker won the Wimbledon for the third time and an eight-year-old boy called Roger Federer was ecstatic seeing his idol win.

A young German driver called Michael Schumacher signed on for his first season of Formula 3 racing that year, which he won the next year, paving his way for a F1 debut a few years later.

In that same month, a teenaged Sachin Tendulkar walked on to an international cricket pitch for the first time.

Only when you take Sachin Tendulkar out of the boundaries of cricket do you realize how long he has been great. Burdened with accusations of chasing personal records or not winning enough matches, we forget Sachin Tendulkar has been performing miracles for an unbelievably long time!

This will be the sixth World Cup of his career (unprecedented in any sport that has a four-yearly World Cup), in which he has scored more than 30,000 runs in international cricket and will still have the same humility and enthusiasm from two decades back.

Every single time he will walk out to bat, he will break a record—for the highest ODI runs scored, highest Man of the Match awards won, highest number of boundaries, highest number of miles run and even highest number of prayers evoked.

This section is a tribute to the man who is probably the world's greatest cricketer and it is our privilege to have seen him play.

Six Cricketers. Seven Facts. Eight Innings. Nine Records. Ten Dulkar!

3.

6 Stars on Sachin

'I never saw myself play. But I feel this player is playing much the same way I used to play'–Donald Bradman.

The world's greatest batsman actually asked his wife to see Sachin play when the youngster's batting style seemed familiar to him. Mrs Bradman confirmed that the player indeed played the same way.

'You know genius when you see it. And let me tell you, Sachin is pure genius'–Brian Lara

The prodigious scorer from West Indies had a see-saw battle with Sachin going for the title of the highest run-getter ever. Eventually, Sachin won. But the record for the highest individual score (400*) still resides with Lara.

'I would really like to bend down and touch his feet'–Sunil Gavaskar.

The two Little Masters from Mumbai have a mutual admiration society going, exemplified by this statement which Gavaskar made when Sachin scored his ODI double-century.

'I would be disappointed if Sachin does not get a hundred 100s in international cricket'–Shane Warne in 2002.

The world's best leg-spinner is an astute judge of cricketing talent. When he made this prediction, Sachin had 60 centuries. Eight years later, he is just adrift of the target.

'In the next 100 years, you will not witness another Tendulkar. He is a once-in-a-century player'–Muttiah Muralitharan.

World's leading wicket-taker knows what his batting counterpart is all about. And refuses to believe gushing media reports which often discover the 'next Tendulkar'.

4.

7 Things About Sachin You (Probably) Didn't Know!

1. **Sachin scored zeroes in his first two ODI innings.**
   The first was against Pakistan in Gujranwala, where he was dismissed by Waqar Younis. The second was against New Zealand in Dunedin. The Kiwi captain was John Wright, who went on to become India's coach.

2. **Sachin is not only the highest centurion in ODIs. He has the maximum number of 90s (18) as well.**
   In Tests, the maximum 90s record is held jointly by Rahul Dravid and Steve Waugh (10 each).

3. **Among Indian players, Sachin has the highest number of ducks (20) in ODIs. But that's probably because he has played the highest number of innings (430+ and counting). Sanath Jayasuriya who has played a similar number of innings has 34 ducks!**
   But Sachin has never got out on the first ball of the match.

4. **Having scored 17,000+ runs in his ODI career (with nearly 2,000 fours and about 200 sixes), Sachin has physically run nearly 9,000 runs. That's about 180 km. If he started from his home, he would have crossed Pune by now!**

5. **Sachin's long-standing opening partner, Sourav Ganguly, has crossed several 1,000-run barriers faster (i.e. in lesser number of innings) than him. Sourav had reached 1,000, 2,000, 3,000, 4,000, 5,000, 6,000, 7,000, 8,000 and 9,000 runs faster but**

Sachin overtook him at 10,000 and has remained the fastest in the world ever since.

6. Sachin and Lara took exactly the same number of innings—195—to reach 10,000 runs in Tests.
7. Sachin flunked his Class XII Board exams. By six marks.

5.

8 Innings Sachin Special

Sachin Tendulkar has a billion fans in India and therefore, a billion lists of his best innings.

Some innings were plain brilliant. Some have a sentimental value. Some are more significant than they should be, because they started off something bigger.

So, what's your favourite Sachin innings?

1. VS NEW ZEALAND. AUCKLAND, MARCH 1994

The Kiwis scoring a paltry 140 odd and India getting it in less than 24 overs is no big deal. Except that this match was the first time Sachin Tendulkar opened the innings. Coming at No. 5 or 6 some seventy times before this one was a criminal waste of the batsman and nobody felt it more than Sachin himself. He offered his captain and coach a deal—let me open this one time and if I fail, I will never ask you again. They let him open, he scored a blazing 82 off 49 balls (15 fours, 2 sixes) and bowlers the world over are paying for it. Still.

2. VS AUSTRALIA. SHARJAH, APRIL 1998

3. VS AUSTRALIA. SHARJAH, APRIL 1998

These two innings cannot be separated. They came within two days of each other. Against the same team, one of world's best. And they are part of the same story.

In the final league match of the Coca Cola Cup, India had to score 237 in 46 overs against Australia to qualify for the finals. India got to 250, of which Sachin scored 143 (off 131 balls, 9 fours, 5 sixes) and the second highest scorer was Nayan Mongia at 35.

In the final match, Australia set a target of 273. And Sachin took off from where he left in the earlier match. He hit 12 fours and 3 sixes en route to 134 as India won with 9 balls to spare.

4.VS AUSTRALIA. WARM-UP MATCH, MUMBAI, FEBRUARY 1998

This series was billed as the Battle of the Best—Sachin Tendulkar vs Shane Warne. And it started when Sachin led Mumbai, the reigning Ranji Champions, in a warm-up game. In reply to 305, Mumbai scored 410 in, hold your breath, 78 overs. Nearly half those runs came from Sachin (204* in 192 balls, 25 fours, 2 sixes) and Shane Warne went for an embarrassing 111 runs in 16 overs—nearly 7 runs per over! Australia lost the three-day match by 10 wickets.

Everybody saw, and still remembers, Sachin's innings in the Chennai Test later in that series where he demolished Warne. But this is where it had all started.

5. VS PAKISTAN. FIRST TEST, CHENNAI, JANUARY 1999

In a relatively low scoring match, India was required to score 271 in the fourth innings to win. It crumpled to 82/5 in double quick time with the entire top order falling prey to some sharp bowling by Pakistan. Batting with a bad back and the burden of a zero in the first innings, Sachin took India to 254 before he got out for a brilliant 136. We had forgotten how good the Pakistan attack was because the next 3 wickets fell for 4 runs and India crashed to a 17-run defeat. No match underlined India's dependence on Sachin more than this one.

6. VS KENYA. ICC WORLD CUP, MAY 1999

Kenya was not expected to trouble Sachin and they didn't. With Dravid at the other end scoring a century as well, he scored 140 runs off 101 balls, hitting 16 fours and 3 sixes on the way. No big deal. Except Sachin had returned from his father's funeral the day before. He had to rush back to India when his father passed away (after the previous match). He completed the last rites and came back to do what his father wanted him to.

On this day, Sachin ceased to be India's favourite cricketer and became the country's favourite son.

7. VS AUSTRALIA. FOURTH TEST, SYDNEY, JANUARY 2004

The bitter rivalry of India and Australia played out perfectly in this series where India won the second Test, lost the third and came into the final one with Sachin in mediocre form. His string of scores in the series were 0, DNB, 1, 37, 0, 44 while each of India's batsmen had scored at least one stellar innings. Skipper Ganguly had led the charge with a 144 in Brisbane, Dravid (233) and Laxman (148) sealed the deal in Adelaide and Sehwag exploded a 195 in Melbourne. For India to draw or win the series, one batsman needed 'not to get out at all'.

Playing completely differently from his normal style, Sachin hung around for 436 balls in the first innings and scored 241*. He literally ground the bowling to dust as India crossed 700 runs in that innings (with V.V.S. Laxman contributing an elegant 178). And, no, he did not get out at all in that Test. He was not out on 60 in the second innings.

8. VS AUSTRALIA. FIFTH ODI, NOVEMBER 2009

What do you do when the world's best team bats first and scores 350 runs in 50 overs? How do you feel when India keeps losing wickets in the chase and is at 162/4? You ask, 'Is Sachin still there?'

In Suresh Raina's company, Sachin took India to 299 before Raina fell and to 332 before he fell himself. 175 runs in 141 balls (19 fours and 4 sixes) were not enough as the last 3 wickets fell for 15 and India lost by 3 runs.

6.

9 ODI Records to Break in This World Cup

Sachin has pretty much every batting record ticked. There is a handful that still eludes him and this World Cup would be the last chance to get them.

1. MOST RUNS IN ONE ODI SERIES

Current record holder: Greg Chappell scored 686 runs in 14 innings of Benson & Hedges World Series Cup way back in 1980-'81.

Sachin's best attempt: 673 runs in 11 innings of the 2003 World Cup.

Chance in this Cup: 700 runs in the maximum nine games possible, of which three are against newer teams like Bangladesh, Ireland and Netherlands. Quite possible!

While he is at it, he might as well break the record for the most centuries in one series. The current record holder is Desmond Haynes who hit 3 hundreds in 4 innings of a series against Australia in 1983-84. That's like ancient! And in any case, he'll need about 3 centuries if he has to get to 700 runs.

All records updated till November 2010.

2. MOST CONSECUTIVE INNINGS WITH HALF-CENTURIES

Current record holder: Javed Miandad of Pakistan had 9 consecutive innings in between March and May 1987, where he scored fifties.
Sachin's best attempt: Sachin had scored 5 consecutive fifties in November 1994.
Chance in this Cup: 9 consecutive fifties is going to be hell of a difficult thing to do. But with a maximum of nine possible matches, the symmetry is unmistakable!

3. HIGHEST STRIKE RATE IN AN INNINGS

Current record holder: Shahid Afridi, who achieved a strike rate of 305 by scoring 55 runs in 18 balls (against newcomers Netherlands in 2002).
Sachin's best attempt: Strike rate of 197 (57* off 29 balls) against first-timer Bermuda in the 2007 World Cup.
Chance in this Cup: In recent times, Sachin has been more of a sheet anchor instead of a tear-away exploder. But hey, 50 runs in about 15 balls isn't all that difficult.

4. MOST SIXES IN A CAREER

Current record holder: The top three six-hitters of all times are Shahid Afridi (272), Sanath Jayasuriya (270), Sourav Ganguly (190).
Sachin's best attempt: At No. 4, with 185 hits into the stands.
Chance in this Cup: The world record is still going to be with Afridi/Jayasuriya but Sachin may well break the Indian record and overtake Ganguly.

5. HIGHEST OPENING PARTNERSHIP

Current record holder: 286 runs put up by Tharanga and Jayasuriya in 2006, when they forgot to get out against England.
Sachin's best attempt: 258 runs, along with Ganguly against Kenya in 2001. In fact, he has one more 250+ attempt (252), again with Ganguly, against Sri Lanka in 1998.
Chance in this Cup: Opening with either Gambhir or Sehwag, two of the best openers of the world, gives him as good a chance as any.

He already holds the world record for the second and third wicket partnerships. Both with Dravid. Both in 1999. Coupled with the two records with Ganguly, it shows how dominating the troika of Tendulkar-Dravid-Ganguly had been in the late 1990s and early 2000s.

6. HIGHEST FOURTH / FIFTH WICKET PARTNERSHIP

Current record holder: An Indian pair—Mohammed Azharuddin and Ajay Jadeja—hold both the records. The duo scored an astonishing 275 (unbroken) against Zimbabwe for the fourth wicket (in 1998) and 223 against Sri Lanka for the fifth (in 1997).
Sachin's best attempt: En route to his epic 175 against Australia in 2009, Sachin put together 137 runs for the fifth wicket with Suresh Raina. His best for the fourth wicket is 169, along with Rahul Dravid against England in 2002 (one of the earlier matches of the NatWest Trophy).
Chance in this Cup: With M.S. Dhoni as the likely batsman at No. 6 or 7, India has the strongest player in recent times. And with Sachin at the other end, no other pair is more likely to break this record.

But remember one thing, 240 runs for fourth/fifth wicket means a top order collapse!

7. OLDEST PLAYER TO SCORE A CENTURY

Current record holder: When Jayasuriya scored a century in January 2009, he was thirty-nine years and 212 days old.
Sachin's best attempt: Sachin's last century, actually, the double century, was scored when he was thirty-six years and 306 days old.
Chance in this Cup: Nope. On the date of the 2011 World Cup Finals, Sachin will be thirty-seven years and 343 days old. Forget old fogey Jayasuriya, he won't even be breaking the Indian record held by Sunil Gavaskar, who scored a century at the ripe young age of thirty-eight years and 113 days.

8. 100 FIFTIES

Current record holder: Nobody. Sachin, himself, has scored 93 fifties in ODI cricket. The next in the list is Inzamam Ul-Haq (83 fifties), who has retired from international cricket. Ponting is the highest (79 fifties) among current players.
Sachin's best attempt: As above.
Chance in this Cup: Very difficult. 7 fifties out of nine matches is quite a task.

9. 50 HUNDREDS

Current record holder: Nobody. Sachin, himself, has scored 46 hundreds in ODI cricket. Next in the list is Ricky Ponting, way behind at 29 centuries.
Sachin's best attempt: As above.
Chance in this Cup: Both this record and the previous cannot happen. Take your pick which one you want!

10. SCARY! MOST RUNS ON THE LOSING SIDE

Current record holder: Charles Coventry of Zimbabwe, who scored 194 and still lost to Bangladesh!
Sachin's best attempt: 175 runs against Australia (in November 2009), when the rest of the team collapsed around him.

We hope he doesn't break *this* record at least!

MOUNT 200

Two hundred runs in an ODI is a peak that many people have aspired for, few people have come within sniffing distance of and only the most privileged have managed to scale.

This is a look at the people who have scored 190+ in ODIs, which is a true test of batting skill, patience, stamina and a wee bit of luck.

194, SAEED ANWAR (PAKISTAN) AGAINST INDIA, MAY 1997

India and Pakistan always reserve their best for each other. On a sultry Chennai evening, Pakistani opener Saeed Anwar mounted a tremendous assault and scored a mammoth 194 off only 146 deliveries (with 22 fours and 5 sixes), in the process taking his team to a then-unbeatable score of 327. Coincidentally, he got out to the bowling of Tendulkar while trying to push the run rate even higher in the last overs.

India's chase was spirited but ended 35 runs short as Dravid scored a century, but the bottom order was unable to keep the momentum.

194*, CHARLES COVENTRY (ZIMBABWE) AGAINST BANGLADESH, AUGUST 2009

Coming one-down after an early wicket, Charles Coventry launched into the Bangla bowling attack with a flurry of sixes (7, to be precise) and 16 fours. He reached the score in 156 deliveries and remained not out till the end, taking him a notch above Saeed Anwar and his team to a not-so-massive 312 due to wickets lost at regular intervals.

Such a performance ended with heartbreak as Bangladesh, helped by 154 from opener Tamim Iqbal, chased down the score (with 2 overs to spare) thanks to useful contributions from the entire side.

200*, SACHIN TENDULKAR (INDIA) AGAINST SOUTH AFRICA, FEBRUARY 2010

It had to be him. While many had come close, Sachin Tendulkar seemed to have the *right* to become the first man to score 200 runs in ODIs. Scored off 147 deliveries, Sachin hit 25 boundaries (but only 3 sixes) to reach the landmark in the penultimate over of the innings. For the first time in his life, M.S. Dhoni (who was batting with him at the other end) was booed for hitting fours and not giving Sachin the strike!

The Indian score of 401 was too much for the South Africans, who folded up for 248 despite a century by A.B. de Villiers.

229*, BELINDA CLARK (AUSTRALIA W) AGAINST DENMARK W, DECEMBER 1997

Indeed, Sachin Tendulkar is the first *man* to hit a double-century. The first ODI double-century ever was hit about thirteen years before him by Belinda Clark, then captain of the Australia Women's cricket team. Scored off only 155 balls and with 22 fours (no sixes!), this was against the Denmark Women's team in the Women's World Cup (held in India that year).

Post her innings, Denmark was bundled out for only 49 and the winning margin (363 runs) is again much more than the men's world record (290 runs).

8.

The Teams

Fourteen teams face off in the World Cup.

Some start with formidable reputations with fans expecting them to go the whole distance. Some are just expected to make up the numbers, coming from countries where ICC is trying to popularize the game.

Some teams have stars with records against their name, multi-million dollar incomes and thousands of fans screaming when they come out of airports. Other teams have players who have to apply for leaves from their day jobs—at a bank maybe—to play in the World Cup.

The beauty of the 2011 World Cup, like the previous ones, is that we don't know which team will win on a given day. Like Bangladesh, Kenya and Ireland in the last three World Cups, there will probably be a team who will start the tournament as an underdog but go on to create a few heartbreaks among the bigger guns.

And as a sweet gesture, they will probably take the autographs of their heroes after the win!

The tournament is structured in two groups:

Group A	Test Nations: Australia, New Zealand, Pakistan, Sri Lanka, Zimbabwe ICC Associates: Canada, Kenya
Group B	Test Nations: Bangladesh, England, India, South Africa, West Indies ICC Associates: Ireland, Netherlands

Each group consists of five Test nations (who have qualified automatically) and two ICC associate nations (who are the first four teams from the ICC World Cup Qualifier Trophy).

The top four teams of each group qualify for the knockout round—the quarter-finals. The first placed teams play the third placed teams of the opposing groups while the second placed and fourth placed teams face off.

The winners move on to the semi-finals and then, the final.

GROUP A: AUSTRALIA

Past Record at World Cup	Four-time winner. After the first victory in 1987, Australia has had a hat-trick: 1999, 2003 and 2007 which was their period of dominance in world cricket.
Watch out for!	A new look side playing for the first time without players like Gilchrist, Warne and McGrath who made them the No. 1 team for nearly a decade.
Most likely to	Win it. Despite the gap between them and other teams narrowing, the fabled Aussie spirit and superb fitness make them the team to beat!
Group Matches	21 Feb–Zimbabwe 25 Feb–New Zealand 5 Mar–Sri Lanka 13 Mar–Kenya 16 Mar–Canada 19 Mar–Pakistan

GROUP A: CANADA

Past Record at World Cup	Had three outings in 1979, 2003 and 2007. Has had some success against fellow minnows but have also had a couple of records for the lowest totals ever!
Watch out for!	No major stars. Their wicketkeeper-captain, Ashish Bagai, is of Indian origin and is one of the key players.
Most likely to	They were placed second in the ICC Qualifier, ahead of Kenya whom they should logically beat. If they pull off an upset against Zimbabwe, then they are just one win away from a quarter-final berth.
Group Matches	20 Feb–Sri Lanka 28 Feb–Zimbabwe 3 Mar–Pakistan 7 Mar–Kenya 13 Mar–New Zealand 16 Mar–Australia

GROUP A: KENYA

Past Record at World Cup	Stunningly, semi-finalist in 2003. Have pulled off upsets in 1996 (West Indies) and 2003 (Sri Lanka, Zimbabwe).
Watch out for!	No major stars. All-rounder Thomas Odoyo and batsman Steve Tikolo bring in a lot of experience.
Most likely to	Give a tough fight at the group stage. Maybe good for one upset, at best. Considerably weakened from their earlier peaks when they were a semi-finalist at the 2003 World Cup.

Group Matches	20 Feb–New Zealand 23 Feb–Pakistan 1 Mar–Sri Lanka 7 Mar–Canada 13 Mar–Australia 20 Mar–Zimbabwe

GROUP A: NEW ZEALAND

Past Record at World Cup	Very low-key but consistent team. Has made it to five semi-finals in the last nine Cups.
Watch out for!	Brendon McCullum, the explosive wicketkeeper-batsman, Ross Taylor, another hard-hitter, Jacob Oram, a solid all-rounder and captain Daniel Vettori are all familiar with Indian conditions, having played impressively in IPL. They all have the power to go the distance.
Most likely to	Reach quarter-finals for sure and even the semis, if the draw favours them.
Group Matches	20 Feb–Kenya 25 Feb–Australia 4 Mar–Zimbabwe 8 Mar–Pakistan 13 Mar–Canada 18 Mar–Sri Lanka

GROUP A: PAKISTAN

Past Record at World Cup	Winner in 1992, when it came back from the brink to win. Runners-up in 1999, demolished by Australia in the finals.

Watch out for!	Much of the talented team is in disarray due to allegations of match-fixing, disciplinary issues and injuries. But under Shahid Afridi, Pakistan is likely to do what they do best—win with their backs to the wall.
Most likely to	Should make it to the quarter-finals, barring a major upset (which will also revive fixing allegations). Post which, it depends on the luck of the draw and how well this talented bunch of youngsters rise to the occasion.
Group Matches	23 Feb–Kenya 26 Feb–Sri Lanka 3 Mar–Canada 8 Mar–New Zealand 14 Mar–Zimbabwe 19 Mar–Australia

GROUP A: SRI LANKA

Past Record at World Cup	Winner in 1996 and runners-up in 2007, both finals involving Australia.
Watch out for!	A formidable batting line-up led by Mahela Jayawardene, Tilakaratne Dilshan and captain Kumar Sangakkara. Their bowling may get a surprise boost if Muttiah Muralitharan decides to come out of retirement!
Most likely to	Make semi-finals. On home turf, anything less would be a colossal disappointment.
Group Matches	20 Feb–Canada 26 Feb–Pakistan 1 Mar–Kenya 5 Mar–Australia 10 Mar–Zimbabwe 18 Mar–New Zealand

GROUP A: ZIMBABWE

Past Record at World Cup	Has been playing in every World Cup since 1983, with a few surprise wins and few surprise losses. Has made it to the knockout stages (Super Sixes) in 1999 and 2003.
Watch out for!	No major stars.
Most likely to	Create an upset, at best. Not likely to move beyond the group stage.
Group Matches	21 Feb–Australia 28 Feb–Canada 4 Mar–New Zealand 10 Mar–Sri Lanka 14 Mar–Pakistan 20 Mar–Kenya

GROUP B: BANGLADESH

Past Record at World Cup	The revelation of the 2007 World Cup. Defeated India in the group stages and South Africa in the Super Eights. Pulled off an upset against Pakistan in 1999 as well. Had an ordinary 2003.
Watch out for!	The most rapidly improving team in recent times, who have been coached by Dav Whatmore. Former captain Mohammed Ashraful and Mashrafe Mortza are two key players.
Most likely to	Take advantage of the home conditions. After beating Ireland and Netherlands, if they manage one upset win, they could be in the quarter-finals. West Indies (the weakest team among the top four) would have to be wary of Bangladesh.

Group Matches	19 Feb–India 25 Feb–Ireland 4 Mar–West Indies 11 Mar–England 14 Mar–Netherlands 19 Mar–South Africa

GROUP B: ENGLAND

Past Record at World Cup	England has made it to the finals or semi-finals every single time till 1992, of which three times were runners-up (1979, 1987 and 1992). Yet to make it to the top four after 1992.
Watch out for!	The best English team in recent times, and the reigning T20 World Champions. Experienced hands like Kevin Pietersen, Paul Collingwood and Andrew Strauss will be supported by a very talented group of youngsters.
Most likely to	Get into the quarter-finals for sure, where a favourable draw may even land them into the semi-finals.
Group Matches	22 Feb–Netherlands 27 Feb–India 2 Mar–Ireland 6 Mar–South Africa 11 Mar–Bangladesh 17 Mar–West Indies

GROUP B: INDIA

Past Record at World Cup	Winner of 1983, when nobody expected it to. Runners-up of 2003, where their dream run was stopped by Australia in the final.
Watch out for!	All of them.
Most likely to	Reach semi-finals, at least, by taking advantage of their home base and phenomenal talent.
Group Matches	19 Feb–Bangladesh 27 Feb–England 6 Mar–Ireland 9 Mar–Netherlands 12 Mar–South Africa 20 Mar–West Indies

GROUP B: IRELAND

Past Record at World Cup	Had a very good outing in its first World Cup in 2007, when it defeated Pakistan and Bangladesh.
Watch out for!	No major stars but a team which won the ICC World Cup Qualifier beating more fancied teams.
Most likely to	Unlikely to make quarter-finals but likely to come fifth in the group.
Group Matches	25 Feb–Bangladesh 2 Mar–England 6 Mar–India 11 Mar–West Indies 15 Mar–South Africa 18 Mar–Netherlands

GROUP B: NETHERLANDS

Past Record at World Cup	Certified minnows. The only victory has come against Namibia in 2003 out of four World Cup appearances.
Watch out for!	No major stars. Came third in the ICC World Cup Qualifiers.
Most likely to	Put up a good fight before going down in the group matches.
Group Matches	22 Feb–England 28 Feb–West Indies 3 Mar–South Africa 9 Mar–India 14 Mar–Bangladesh 18 Mar–Ireland

GROUP B: SOUTH AFRICA

Past Record at World Cup	The perennial second favourites and certified chokers. Yet to make it to the finals, though remains most likely to do so. Has lost two incredibly close semi-finals to England (in 1992) and Australia (in 1999). Lost to Australia in the semi-finals in 2007 as well.
Watch out for!	Batsmen like Graeme Smith, Herschelle Gibbs, J.P. Duminy and A.B. de Villiers, all-rounders like Albie Morkel bowlers like Makhaya Ntini and Dale Steyn. Talented, tough and familiar with Indian conditions (thanks to the IPL experience).

Most likely to	Anything less than a semi-final spot would be under-achieving for this formidable team.
Group Matches	24 Feb–West Indies 3 Mar–Netherlands 6 Mar–England 12 Mar–India 15 Mar–Ireland 19 Mar–Bangladesh

GROUP B: WEST INDIES

Past Record at World Cup	The kings of the first two World Cups before going on a terrible slide. After two wins in 1975 and 1979 and runners-up in 1983, has made it to only one semi-final (1996).
Watch out for!	IPL king Kieron Pollard will come in with all guns blazing. He will receive batting support from Kieran Powell and Chris Gayle as well but the team is nowhere the peaks it once ruled.
Most likely to	Reach quarter-finals and end there, unless they pull off an upset to go one more step.
Group Matches	24 Feb–South Africa 28 Feb–Netherlands 4 Mar–Bangladesh 11 Mar–Ireland 17 Mar–England 20 Mar–India

GROUP A

PLAYING SCHEDULE AND PREDICTOR

		Venue		Score			Score	Prediction	Winner
20 Feb	Sunday	Chennai	New Zealand		v	Kenya			
20 Feb	Sunday	Hambantota	Sri Lanka		v	Canada			
21 Feb	Monday	Ahmedabad	Australia		v	Zimbabwe			
23 Feb	Wednesday	Hambantota	Pakistan		v	Kenya			
25 Feb	Friday	Nagpur	New Zealand		v	Australia			
26 Feb	Saturday	Colombo	Sri Lanka		v	Pakistan			
28 Feb	Monday	Nagpur	Zimbabwe		v	Canada			
1 Mar	Tuesday	Colombo	Sri Lanka		v	Kenya			
3 Mar	Thursday	Colombo	Pakistan		v	Canada			
4 Mar	Friday	Ahmedabad	New Zealand		v	Zimbabwe			
5 Mar	Saturday	Colombo	Sri Lanka		v	Australia			
7 Mar	Monday	Delhi	Kenya		v	Canada			
8 Mar	Tuesday	Kandy	Pakistan		v	New Zealand			
10 Mar	Thursday	Kandy	Sri Lanka		v	Zimbabwe			
13 Mar	Sunday	Bengaluru	Australia		v	Kenya			
13 Mar	Sunday	Mumbai	New Zealand		v	Canada			

GROUP B

PLAYING SCHEDULE AND PREDICTOR									
		Venue		**Score**			**Score**	**Prediction**	**Winner**
14 Mar	Monday	Kandy	Pakistan		v	Zimbabwe			
16 Mar	Wednesday	Bengaluru	Australia		v	Canada			
18 Mar	Friday	Mumbai	Sri Lanka		v	New Zealand			
19 Mar	Saturday	Colombo	Pakistan		v	Australia			
20 Mar	Sunday	Kolkata	Zimbabwe		v	Kenya			
19 Feb	Saturday	Dhaka	India		v	Bangladesh			
22 Feb	Tuesday	Nagpur	England		v	Netherlands			
24 Feb	Thursday	Delhi	South Africa		v	West Indies			
25 Feb	Friday	Dhaka	Bangladesh		v	Ireland			
27 Feb	Sunday	Kolkata	India		v	England			
28 Feb	Monday	Delhi	West Indies		v	Netherlands			
2 Mar	Wednesday	Bengaluru	England		v	Ireland			
3 Mar	Thursday	Mohali	South Africa		v	Netherlands			
4 Mar	Friday	Dhaka	Bangladesh		v	West Indies			
6 Mar	Sunday	Bengaluru	India		v	Ireland			

GROUP B

PLAYING SCHEDULE AND PREDICTOR									
		Venue		Score			Score	Prediction	Winner
6 Mar	Sunday	Chennai	England		v	South Africa			
9 Mar	Wednesday	Delhi	India		v	Netherlands			
11 Mar	Friday	Chittagong	Bangladesh		v	England			
11 Mar	Friday	Mohali	Ireland		v	West Indies			
12 Mar	Saturday	Nagpur	India		v	South Africa			
14 Mar	Monday	Chittagong	Bangladesh		v	Netherlands			
15 Mar	Tuesday	Kolkata	South Africa		v	Ireland			
17 Mar	Thursday	Chennai	England		v	West Indies			
18 Mar	Friday	Kolkata	Ireland		v	Netherlands			
19 Mar	Saturday	Dhaka	Bangladesh		v	South Africa			
20 Mar	Sunday	Chennai	India		v	West Indies			

POINTS TALLY

	Australia	Canada	Kenya	New Zealand	Pakistan	Sri Lanka	Zimbabwe	POINTS
Australia								
Canada								
Kenya								
New Zealand								
Pakistan								
Sri Lanka								
Zimbabwe								

	Bangladesh	England	India	Ireland	Netherlands	South Africa	West Indies	POINTS
Bangladesh								
England								
India								
Ireland								
Netherlands								
South Africa								
West Indies								

A1	
A2	
A3	
A4	

B1	
B2	
B3	
B4	

KNOCKOUTS

23 March DHAKA

A1	
B3	

24 March COLOMBO

A2	
B4	

25 March DHAKA

A4	
B2	

26 March AHMEDABAD

A3	
B1	

29 March COLOMBO

Winner of 23 March	
Winner of 24 March	

30 March MOHALI

Winner of 25 March	
Winner of 26 March	

2 April MUMBAI

Winner of 29 March	
Winner of 30 March	

FUNNY SCORES

There are some scores in cricket on which people have spent lots of think-time. Names have been thought of, connections discovered and even superstitions started.

These are obviously separate from the 100s and 50s with which we are all rightly obsessed!

ZERO

Quite obviously, this is the number which has caused the maximum heartburn among sportsmen and commentators alike.

The common term for the score, 'duck', originates from the phrase 'duck's egg' which is what a zero looks like! Maybe the term was originated to spare the batsman the ignominy of a 'zero' but Australian television made the matter worse by designing a cartoon character (called Daddles) which fretted, fumed and walked back to the pavilion on screen along with the despondent batsman.

The only thing worse than a zero is a zero in the second innings as well! And there are names for different degrees of failure.

A **pair** is a batsman scoring a zero in both innings of a Test match. This gets worse with a **King's pair**—a zero scored in both innings, out first ball both times. And that's not all. An **Emperor's pair** is something that is the fate of even fewer people. It is when an opener gets out first ball in both innings. Nothing, absolutely nothing, can get worse than that!

NELSON

The score of 111 is assigned a 'bad luck charm' for no apparent reason. In fact, no misfortune, in the form of getting out or even getting injured, has befallen any batsman when he has been on 111.

The most visible victim of this superstition was umpire David Shepherd. Despite his considerable weight, he skipped on one leg after every delivery that kept the team score at 111.

There is an interesting, and faulty, story behind how the score started being called 'Nelson'. It was named after Admiral Horatio Nelson (the British naval hero, whose statue graces Trafalgar Square of London), who was supposed to have one leg, one arm and one eye. The connection is brilliant except that the poor Admiral had both his legs. So he could well have skipped when his team's score touched 111!

In some very obscure circles (probably witch doctors, not cricketers!), even the score of 87 is considered unlucky because it is 13 short of a century. Did somebody tell these people that maybe they should start with designating the score of 13 unlucky in the first place?

PART C

Odds and Ends

1.

Neighbourhood Cricket

Cricket goes beyond the twenty-two yards of the cricket pitch. Overwhelming amounts of cricket gets played all around us. We play it every day. And we let the game play us.

In the lane outside our house. On a computer screen near us. In Bollywood. On Playstations and Xbox-es. Sometimes, we even play cricket inside the classroom while a teacher drones on!

This section is about the cricket that gets played outside stadiums and without floodlights–but with as much passion. This is the cricket where you and I are heroes.

And therefore, it is as interesting as the real thing. Sometimes it is more interesting than the real thing!

GALI CRICKET

The nursery of cricket has always been the *mohalla* (neighbourhood).

In India (and Pakistan as well), a lot of cricket is first played in *galis* (lanes) as both these countries never had very high quality sporting facilities. West Indies has beaches where boys grow up playing cricket. Australia and England, by and large, have been fortunate enough to have proper grounds to play cricket in.

In India, Shivaji Park in the Dadar area of Mumbai has been something like a nursery of cricketers. This is a big field where hundreds of boys practise cricket and Dadar can justifiably claim to be the 'nursery of Indian cricket'. Generations of Mumbai cricketers have perfected their skills in and around this locality.

However, the majority of the sport is not played in an organized maidan but with a tennis ball in the neighbourhood. And gali cricket's first rule is that no two localities can have the same set of rules!

All rules of scoring and dismissal are dependent on the topography of the playing field. Pillars, trees, railings are all assigned a certain score should the ball hit them. If you are playing on a basketball court, for example, the standard score for hitting the basket-board is 12 runs!

Most mohallas have uneven talent. Think about your own team—there are one or two very good players, one guy who has the bat (and therefore, has to be given 'batting') and rest are there to make up numbers! So, we have to identify strange rules (sometimes to strengthen teams and sometimes to weaken them).

Last Man Batting: If one team has one player less than the other, then the not-out batsman gets to bat out the remaining deliveries.

One-Drop-One-Hand: Typically in underarm games, if a fielder takes a one-handed catch after the ball has bounced once, then the batsman is given out. This is never as easy as it sounds because the reflex is always to take the ball with both hands!

In different parts of the world, including India, there are many variations of local cricket, just in case the original version gets boring!

TAPE-BALL CRICKET

Hugely popular in Pakistan, this is played with a tennis ball covered with insulation tape. The tape covers the entire ball except for a short gap. This gap is what causes the ball to swing. All local cricket in Pakistan is played with this ball and is widely accepted as the reason why the country consistently produces such high-quality fast bowlers. Apart from the strength required to bowl consistently, the addition of the tape makes the ball do strange things. It gives the bowler power like no other version of gali cricket, where the odds are usually in the batsman's favour.

FRENCH CRICKET

There is no reason for calling this version 'French'—because it has nothing to do with France!

The batsman stands with his feet together and the bat in front of his legs. His feet are the 'stumps' and there are only three ways to get out—bowled (which is also LBW!), caught, and if his feet move. The batsman can score runs by revolving the bat around his body, passing it from one hand to another.

In a variation, whichever fielder fields the ball can bowl the next delivery, though the batsman cannot turn his feet but only adjust his waist to face the bowler.

2.

Armchair Cricket

For those who are not very interested in running around, working up a sweat and playing the real thing, several versions of cricket exist that require very little equipment and even less effort.

These are ideal games when rain stops play or Sidhu's commentary becomes too much to bear or on a long drive when you can't catch the commentary on the radio.

BOOK CRICKET

The most popular and least resource-intensive version requires a book of medium thickness (to play with) and some stationery (to keep score).

Players: 1+

Game Play: You score runs by flipping the pages of the book.

The last digit of the page number on the left-hand indicates the score. A last digit of 2 means 1, 4 means 2, 6 means 3, 8 means 4, a blank page means 6 and zero means out. One team plays out his innings and gives the other guy a chance. Simple.

You can twist this scoring rule to suit yourself. For example, if you are looking at a high-scoring match, you should take 0 as a sixer and a blank page as out.

Variations: A single player can play himself. Multiple players can form teams and a proper batting order (though that's no guarantee of the opener scoring more than the last man!). Opposing teams may use the same or different books. Different players may arrive with their own 'lucky books'.

Cheat Notes: Shady players are known to mark the 4/6 pages on the edge of a book.

CALCULATOR CRICKET

This is the high-tech version of book-cricket.

Game Play: You use the randomizer function of a scientific calculator or in Microsoft Excel.

By using the function RAND in MS Excel, one can generate a series of random numbers. The last digit of the random number is used to indicate the run scored. For example, last digits of 1, 2, 3, 4 and 6 can be equal to runs scored. 5, 7, 8 and 9 can count as dot balls. Zero can still be out.

All variations of book cricket can be tried out here as well, but try cheating in this one!

CARDS CRICKET

The perfect game to turn to when you are simply bored of playing Screw or Rummy with your pack of cards.

Game Play: A pack of cards (or more) is shuffled and cards are picked to determine the scoring.

A pack of cards is shuffled and divided equally between two players (or teams), one of whom is batting and the other fielding.

The cards are ordered from A as lowest (1) to King as highest (13). Each team reveals one unseen card from its pile. The difference between the cards makes up the scores.

If the batting team draws a card higher than the fielding team, then the incremental score (up to a maximum of six) is considered as runs. If the fielding team draws a higher card, differences up to six are considered as non-scoring and differences more than six are taken as dismissals.

3.

Fantasy Cricket

When most cricket tournaments are on, cricket websites run a Fantasy Cricket League. In this format, people can make their own teams (out of those playing in the tournament) and the players get runs or wickets based on their actual performance. So, if you can predict the player who would do well in a match, you can pick him ahead of others and have your 'team' score higher.

But we don't always need a tournament to play Fantasy Cricket. We can choose from any team in the world. In fact, we can choose from any team in the world from any era! Better still, the teams can be chosen as per any connecting link we like.

So, we can have an Asia XI playing Rest of the World. We can have a Left-Handed XI playing the Right-Handed XI. We can have a mini-league of India teams from different ages—India 80s vs India 90s vs India 00s.

Sounds fun?

Let's start off with the last one and make three India teams—one from each decade. How do we decide which player goes where?

You can also decide if your fantasy team will play Tests or ODIs. Or T20. Or if they will play on a spinning track in India or a fast pitch in Australia.

To make every list, you need to set rules beforehand and can't change them for anything. For this list, we will assign players to the decades they started playing in. For example, Gautam Gambhir started playing in the 2000s and will belong to India 00. Since the number of players in India 80 will be a little on the lower side, we will allow players who started playing in the 70s also in this team. Okay?

So, here are the players who fit in each slot for each decade. There are about 15–20 names in the shortlist. From these, you have to choose 11. And why only these? You can add your favourites as well. That's the fun part. Choose anybody. BUT they have to match your initial rule.

	India 80	India 90	India 00
Openers (2)	K. Srikkanth. Sunil Gavaskar. Sachin Tendulkar. N.S. Sidhu.	Sourav Ganguly Virender Sehwag. S. Ramesh	Gautam Gambhir. Wasim Jaffer. Murali Vijay.

All-rounder / Batsman (3)	Kapil Dev. Mohinder Amarnath. Dilip Vengsarkar. Ravi Shastri. Mohammed Azharuddin.	Rahul Dravid. V.V.S. Laxman. Ajay Jadeja. Vinod Kambli. Praveen Amre.	Yuvraj Singh. Rohit Sharma. Robin Uthappa. Virat Kohli.
Wicketkeeper (1)	Syed Kirmani. Kiran More.	Nayan Mongia. Rahul Dravid.	M.S. Dhoni. Parthiv Patel.
Spinners (2)	Maninder Singh. L. Sivaramakrishnan. S. Venkataraghavan. B.S. Bedi.	Anil Kumble. Harbhajan Singh. Sunil Joshi.	Amit Mishra. Ramesh Powar.
Fast bowlers (3)	Yashpal Sharma. Roger Binny. Manoj Prabhakar.	Javagal Srinath. Venkatesh Prasad. Zaheer Khan. Ajit Agarkar.	Ashish Nehra. L. Balaji. Irfan Pathan. R.P. Singh.

The number in brackets indicates the recommended number to be chosen for a balanced team. But don't let that restrict you. If your team is playing in Brisbane, you can choose five pacers!

Now let's try another face-off. One between left-handers and right-handers. Let the first teams be from India. Then you can go ahead and make a World XI.

	Right-handers	Left-handers
Openers (2)	The left-handers are the difficult list to crack. Among right-handers, you have the problem of plenty!	Sourav Ganguly. Gautam Gambhir.
All-rounder / Batsman (3)		Yuvraj Singh. Vinod Kambli. Robin Singh. Suresh Raina.
Wicketkeeper (1)		Parthiv Patel.
Spinners (2)		Ravi Shastri. Dilip Doshi. Murali Kartik. Sunil Joshi.
Fast bowlers (3)		Irfan Pathan. Zaheer Khan. Ashish Nehra.

Hey, where do we put people who are ambidextrous? For example, Ganguly is a left-handed batsman but a right-handed bowler. Well, my rule is that he must fit in the position he is chosen for. So, Ganguly is in the opener's slot. You don't agree? Well, make your own rule then!

The most popular thing to do is an All-Time XI. Imagine an India team drawn from the best players down the ages playing a similar star-studded team from Pakistan. Oh, the audience it will get!

Go on, do it!

And you will be in great company since the big daddies of world cricket like this sort of things. We have had some instances in which formal cricket matches have been organized between a World XI and a certain country.

In Oct 2005, ICC organized a Super Series (of 3 ODIs and one Test match) between Australia (the then No. 1 team in ICC rankings) and a World XI chosen by cricket experts around the world. The ODI team was chosen from the following giants:

World XI—Chris Gayle, Kumar Sangakkara, Virender Sehwag, Jacques Kallis, Brian Lara (vice-captain), Rahul Dravid, Kevin Pietersen, Andrew Flintoff, Shahid Afridi, Shaun Pollock (captain), Daniel Vettori, Shoaib Akhtar, Chris Gayle, Muttiah Muralitharan, Makhaya Ntini.[1]

Result? Australia won all four matches!

That was easy since they actually *played*. But how are the fantasy matches settled? Who wins? Who loses?

Well, you could do the logical thing by logging on to Cricinfo and checking their batting averages. The team with the higher total of batting averages wins. Or you could do it the fun way—get a friend to make his XI and then argue with him till he gives up!

'Your team sucks!'

'No, YOUR team sucks!'

---

[1] Sachin Tendulkar could not participate due to injuries.

4.

Cricket Books and Films

What do you do when there are long gaps between the India matches? What do you do when a match finishes early and you still haven't had your fill of cricket for the evening? What do you do—God forbid—if India is knocked out of the World Cup?

Here is a selection of some great books and films on cricket that are sometimes more gripping than the real thing. For addicts, this is a fix of a different kind.

LAGAAN

Foreign coach, check. Match-fixing, check. The doosra, check. Coloured clothing, check. All that is commonplace in modern cricket actually started two centuries back. Bhuvan of Champaner village accepted the challenge of an English army captain and agreed that the result of a cricket match will decide whether the villagers will pay three times their normal tax or remain tax-free for three years. Aamir Khan played the role of the courageous villager, who leads his rag-tag team in a match like no other.

Lagaan was among the five films nominated for the Best Foreign Film Oscar in 2002.

Directed by: Ashutosh Gowariker

Starring: Aamir Khan, Gracy Singh, Rachel Shelley, Paul Blackthorne and others.

IQBAL

Every cricketer worth his salt dreams of wearing the blue uniform with those magical five letters on the chest—I.N.D.I.A. It doesn't really matter if the cricketer cannot speak or hear, as long as he has the guts to follow his dreams. Iqbal was the fast bowler from a village in Andhra Pradesh, who battled his disability, his father's opposition and politics in national cricket to get to his dream. He had a supportive mother and sister as well as a former fast bowler as his coach. But was that enough?

In his debut, Shreyas Talpade played the title role and became a star.

Directed by: Nagesh Kukunoor

Starring: Shreyas Talpade, Naseeruddin Shah, Girish Karnad, Shweta Prasad and others.

BODYLINE

One of the most controversial contests of all time was filmed as a fictional TV series in graphic detail, dwelling on the intricate planning and cold aggression of the English captain Douglas Jardine in an obsessive quest to contain a batsman called Donald Bradman. The obsession, the fears, the ambitions and the passion of the cricketers were brought out in nail-biting detail.

Starring: Hugo Weaving, Gary Sweet and others

SWAMI AND FRIENDS, R.K. NARAYAN

A classic of world fiction, this book follows ten-year-old Swaminathan and his friends, as they bond, fight with each other, get harassed by teachers and, of course, form a cricket team. Set in the town of Malgudi, Swami becomes a deadly fast bowler and a regular member of the MCC (Malgudi Cricket Club).

SPIN AND OTHER TURNS, RAMACHANDRA GUHA

Ramachandra Guha has been blessed with a beautiful writing style, a great memory, a brilliant sense of humour and love for cricket. In this book, he goes back to the great Indian cricketers and his personal memories of them. Many of us wouldn't have seen Sunil Gavaskar, Gundappa Vishwanath or Kapil Dev play, but this book brings them alive.

IDOLS, SUNIL GAVASKAR

One of the greatest batsmen of the world lists down the players he thinks are the greatest. Being an accomplished writer, he manages to detail their cricketing prowess very well and recounts interesting off-the-field episodes too. If the characters from this book formed a World XI, they would be impossible to beat!

TOBY JONES SERIES, MICHAEL PANCKRIDGE

This series of books stars Toby Jones, a talented young cricketer who has gifts other than cricket. He can travel back in time to great cricket matches. In between playing cricket for his local team and managing to hold his own against others, Toby's adventures stretch from the 1930 Ashes series, right down to the 1999 World Cup. What would you give to see Bradman batting live?

JOHN WRIGHT'S INDIAN SUMMERS, JOHN WRIGHT WITH SHARDA UGRA

The autobiography of India's most successful cricket coach is full of great cricketing insights and laced with a fantastic sense of humour. It is a fascinating journey from being a sales manager for cakes to the coach of the world's most cricket-crazy nation.

5.

Cricket on a Different Screen

The popularity of cricket means that it is not only a sport to be played in your gali, in the stadium or to be watched on TV, but you could play its many avatars online as well. Serious cricket websites as well as the hardcore gaming sites have a whole gamut of online cricket games.

And when all else fails (read: the broadband connection is down), there are Xbox and PS3. There are some cool cricket games to play on those as well.

Here is a list. It is hardly complete. Add your own favourites as well!

FANTASY CRICKET

The most popular version of cricket online, drawing millions of fans worldwide, is Fantasy Cricket. You choose your team, usually by choosing players within a total team budget (where prices of players vary daily, based on their recent performances). Mid-way trade-offs are done to exchange the non-performing players for potentially better ones.

www.fantasy.cricinfo.com
www.games2win.com
www.cricket.zapak.com

VIDEO GAMES

Ashes Cricket 2009
Brian Lara International Cricket 2007
International Cricket 2010
Available for: PlayStation 3 and Xbox 360

6.

Cricketers Online

More and more cricketers are going online to connect with fans, discuss sports or just to hang out. The most common den is Twitter. With its 140 characters-per-post limit, our cricketers are adapting well and quickly churning out 'Just back from the gym. Tired. Will win the Cup.' tweets. Some of the savvier ones are also on Facebook. Some have their own websites.

Here is a quick ready-reckoner of who's where, doing what.

MAHENDRA SINGH DHONI

India's captain has at least three homes on Twitter, each of them with a large number of followers, and a few celebrity ones as well!

http://twitter.com/MahendraDhoni - 31,000+ followers. Last update Oct 09.

http://twitter.com/msdhonis - with no updates and 29,000 fans, this is the most bizarre site!

http://twitter.com/MSDmahi - Probably the real one, followed by Mandira Bedi, among others! 20,000+ followers.

SACHIN TENDULKAR

Like he does so often on the cricket field, Sachin debuted on Twitter and www.twitter.com/sachin_rt became the rage. With nearly 7,00,000 followers, he has left most people far behind, including the other Indian icon @iamsrk.

SHANE WARNE

The world's greatest leg-spinner is also a poker addict and his Twitter handle reflects that. The bio at www.twitter.com/warne888 says 'father to my lovely 3 children, motto keep smiling, be true to yourself'.

His official site is www.shanewarne.com.

VIRENDER SEHWAG

The explosive opener has a solid online following as well. www.twitter.com/sehwagvirender has nearly 60,000 followers who eagerly lap up updates on his visits to a bat factory in Meerut, naming of his son (Vedhant) and watching *A Team: The Movie*.

His official site is www.sehwagworld.com.

OTHER INDIAN CRICKETERS

www.twitter.com/yuvsingh09—Yuvraj Singh

www.twitter.com/ImZaheer—Zaheer Khan, who calls himself 'Fast spin bowler'.

www.twitter.com/ImRo45—Rohit Sharma. Used Cristiano Ronaldo as his profile pic during the football World Cup.

www.twitter.com/ImRaina—Suresh Raina.

http://twitter.com/harbhajan_singh—Harbhajan Singh also has an official website (www.bhajjiworld.com) and a Facebook page (http://www.facebook.com/pages/Harbhajan-Singh-Official-Page/119093531456394)

http://twitter.com/gambhirgauti—Gautam Gambhir calls himself 'gamer, car lover, Indian cricket player' and is also on Facebook (http://www.facebook.com/pages/Gautam-Gambhir-Official/134331233249176)

COMMENTATORS

At 35,000 followers, www.twitter.com/bhogleharsha leads the pack with regular updates and good humour.

Another senior journalist—Ayaz Memon—operates from www.twitter.com/cricketwallah and is an authoritative commentator.

If you are looking for lighter stuff, you will have lots of company among the 29,000 people who follow http://twitter.com/mandybedi.

Read More in Puffin

ON TOP OF THE WORLD: MY EVEREST ADVENTURE

Arjun Vajpai

There was a statue of the Buddha at the summit, placed there by the Sherpas. I knelt down and bowed in front of it. I felt complete. When I looked around I felt I ruled the world, with the Himalayas stretching out below me and nothing to obstruct my view.

A month after he had set out, sixteen-year-old Arjun Vajpai stood on top of the world, having conquered Mount Everest. At that time he was the youngest non-Sherpa person in the world to do so. He remains the youngest Indian to have climbed the peak. It had indeed been a long journey. Arjun's fascination with mountains began at the age of ten, nurtured and encouraged by his parents, teachers, and close friends. As a trekker and an athlete, he had trained and worked hard to achieve this amazing feat of endurance.

This is Arjun's story in his own words. Accompany him on an adventure of a lifetime; read about his incredible ascent; and learn what it takes to be a mountaineer. *On Top of the World* is an unforgettable story of inspiration, fortitude and courage; of having a seemingly impossible dream and daring to chase it.

ALL ABOUT ROCKETS

S.K. Das

Who invented rockets?
Why do we need them?
How do rockets work?

It may be rocket science, but it has never been easier to know all about rockets! Through 75 Q & As, you will learn absolutely everything about rockets.

Who makes them?
How are they made?
Who were the scientists who developed the science of rockets?
What will the rockets of the future be like?

These are just some of the fascinating questions answered in this book in easy-to-understand, jargon-free language. Accompanied by numerous illustrations, photographs and suggested experiments which will help you comprehend the principles of rocket science right in your home, *All About Rockets* tells all you ever wanted to know about these intriguing machines.

PUFFIN LIVES: AKBAR, THE MIGHTY EMPEROR

Kavitha Mandana

The birth of a prince in medieval India was usually followed by grand celebrations. Camped out in the wilderness when the news of Akbar's safe delivery reached him, Humayun could only enjoy a quiet moment of thanksgiving. He broke a musk pod and, as the fragrance wafted all over the camp, the new father hoped his son's fame would similarly spread across the world.

Akbar—emperor, warrior, statesman and thinker—is acknowledged as one of the most charismatic personalities in Indian history. Crowned the king of Hindustan at the age of thirteen, his empire expanded to include the farthest corners of the country. Yet he was not just a conqueror. A humanist, Akbar's deep interest in literature, architecture, art, and his inclusive vision of religions at a time when such thoughts were not in fashion, set him down as one of history's most remarkable men.

In this story of his life, as exciting and thrilling as any adventure tale, the author describes Akbar's rough, difficult childhood spent on the run; his consolidation of the empire through war and diplomacy; the myriad interesting and entertaining people who made up his court; the strong women of the Mughal household; and, finally, the intriguing circumstances under which the crown passed on to his son, Jehangir. Accompanied by many interesting facts about the Mughal empire and the world in the 16th century, this book is a fascinating introduction to the life and times of an emperor who still rules our imaginations.

PUFFIN LIVES: MAHATMA GANDHI, THE FATHER OF THE NATION

Subhadra Sen Gupta

On his passport he was Mohandas Karamchand Gandhi. The poet Rabindranath Tagore gave him the title 'Mahatma', the great soul, but he was rather uncomfortable with that. Nelson Mandela calls him a 'sacred warrior', others describe him as the 'the saint of the spinning wheel' and we now declare him as our 'Father of the Nation'.

A courageous freedom fighter, a shrewd politician, a passionate social reformer and a staunch nationalist, Mahatma Gandhi was all this and much more. He was the most unusual leader this country has seen, and one of the most influential personalities whose name is synonymous with India's independence. He was the one who touched the lives of millions, whose ideals of satyagraha and ahimsa inspired great leaders of the world, and who could make the entire country come to a halt by going on a fast.

Through a vivid narrative, author Subhadra Sen Gupta recreates the life and legacy of this phenomenal leader to portray the man beneath the simple handspun clothes, who ate saltless vegetables and bitter neem chutney; who greeted kings and paupers alike; who walked 240 miles at the age of sixty to break the Salt Law; and whose entire life was dedicated to truth and to peace. Even today as we read inspirational accounts of Gandhiji's life and talk of *gandhigiri*, we know that his ideals are alive and relevant to today's generation.